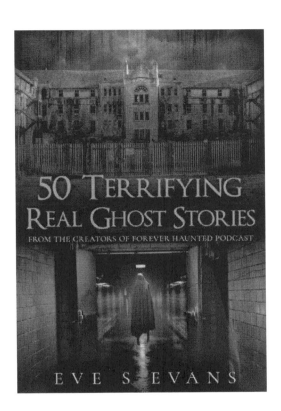

50 TERRIFYING
REAL GHOST STORIES

FROM THE CREATORS OF FOREVER HAUNTED PODCAST

EVE S. EVANS

Shadow people are a projection of our worst nightmares. Everyone has had a nightmare at one point of their life. But what if that nightmare was crouched next to your bed watching you sleep? A figure so terrifyingly darker than the unlit surroundings of your room. Shadow Beings come in different shapes and sizes. Some are horrid looking and stare on for what seems like an eternity, while others are misty-like and disappear in the blink of an eye. 15 spine-chilling tales of shadow entity encounters, sure to leave you awake past dawn.

★ ★ ★ ★ ★ "Absolutely Gripping." - Dayna S.

★ ★ ★ ★ "A Captivating Page-Turner." - Mike B.

★ ★ ★ ★ ★ "Worthy if it's own podcast." - James Curro

★ ★ ★ ★ ★ "The Twilight Zone meets Tales From the Crypt." - Liz J.

PARANORMAL STORIES OF HAUNTED HOTELS

20 creepy chapters to leave you craving more, from author Eve S Evans and R. Harrell.

Hotels are a place that some people frequent. Business trips, conferences, get-a-ways, and vacations. But these people have stories to share from their experiences at hotels that weren't quite what they expected...

As one patron has advised after a terrifying experience, if you are going to an unfamiliar area, ask about the history of the place before you stay there...

A Business trip with an unexpected ghostly twist and many others. Some hotel employees as well as patrons recount numerous terrifying paranormal experiences in Haunted Hotels.

★ ★ ★ ★ ★ "Absolutely Gripping." - Dayna S.

★ ★ ★ ★ "A Captivating Page-Turner." - Mike B.

★ ★ ★ ★ ★ "Worthy if it's own podcast." - James Curro

★ ★ ★ ★ ★ "The Twilight Zone meets Tales From the Crypt." - Liz J.

REAL CREEPY STORIES OF PARANORMAL ITEMS
HAUNTED
OBJECTS

Ever buy something second hand only to bring it home and notice odd things start to occur? After inheriting something old, did you start to feel off or watched? How about hearing or seeing things that just cannot be explained?

In this anthology of paranormal stories you will read about the most wicked hauntings that are assumed to be caused by haunted objects.

REAL GHOST STORIES
PARALYZING TALES OF
PARANORMAL ENCOUNTERS

After befriending a local homeless man, Annie begins having extreme paranormal activity in her apartment. Read more in: The Beggar.
Roger and his wife have saved for ages for the perfect home. Finally, they find an amazing deal on a local foreclosure. But what terrifying secrets are beyond its walls? Read more in: A Steal of A Deal.
Every summer is the highlight of her summer vacation when she gets to visit her grandparents for a few weeks. This summer is different. Something is lurking at her grandparent's home… waiting. Read more in: The Shadow Man.
Ever been scared in the middle of the night? Ever been fearful of the dark and what lies in wait? This young girl and her brother have an experience to last a lifetime. Read more in: Fear In The Hallway.

Delve into these stories and twenty more delectable paranormal encounters from paranormal horror author Eve S. Evans.

★ ★ ★ ★ ★ "Thank you so much for this book. It has helped me feel much better about what I'm going through. Thanks again!" – P. Jewels

PARANORMAL PLACES
A JOURNEY INTO SOME OF THE
WORLD'S MOST HAUNTED LOCATIONS

Take your mind on a historic journey. Explore the stories and legends behind some of the world's most paranormal locations. Some of the tales you will find in this book involve: bloody apparitions, residual hauntings, objects moving by unseen forces, unexplainable temperature changes, entities on stairwells, a cursed road, a dungeon that held one hundred and fifty bodies and multiple other phenomenon.

★ ★ ★ ★ ★ "Facinating." – R Harrell

★ ★ ★ ★ ★ "Paranormal history at it's finest."
– James Curro

VOICES FROM BEYOND
AN ANTHOLOGY OF LOVED ONES
WHO HAVE ATTEMPTED CONTACT
AFTER DEATH

A delicious assortment of enlightening paranormal anthologies for the supernatural enthusiast. These stories are a variety of true narratives from around the world where people believe they have been visited by either friends, family, lovers, or pets after death. After her twin's untimely passing, unexplained events begin to occur. With a broken heart she tries to mend the best she can. In the beginning, she shrugs off all of the unusual occurrences until she is forced to confront them head on and open her eyes to possibility. Maybe her twin is communicating with her from beyond. Read more in: A Twinly Goodbye. Barely out of high school, Lisa is thrown a curveball when her father suddenly passes. With her life now in utter chaos, he journeys to them with a message from beyond to ease the burden. Read more in: Daddy's Little Girl. A confusing late-night dream foretells of a saddening tragedy linked to their

grandfather. Read more in: You Will Be Fine.
After twelve years of love and memories,
Anna had to bite the bullet and let her beloved
Pomeranian go. But did she ever really leave?
Anna begins to wonder after seeing and
feeling unexplained events. Read more in:
Here to Stay. A simple trip to the grocery store
ended in absolute heartbreak after crossing
paths with a drunk driver. With a shattered
heart, she lets him go and slowly tries to heal.
But it seems as if her son is not ready to go
just yet. The first signs she ignores, but after a
while she has no choice but to open her mind
up to the possibility that he has never really
left. Read more in: I Had to Let You Go.

★ ★ ★ ★ ★ "A light-hearted paranormal
binge." – Trace N.

★ ★ ★ ★ ★ "Some of the stories actually
made me tear up! I loved it!" – Brynn S.

★ ★ ★ ★ "Excellent." -Jorden P.

The following stories are based on true events. Based does not intend to mean they are completely true events. Some of the stories in this book are from fact and some hearsay or stories told about a person, place, or thing over the years.

November © 2020 Eve S. Evans

Cover By: WarrenDesign

DEDICATION:

This book is dedicated to my Christina.
You are such a sweetheart and I'm glad
to have you in my life.

This book contains a collaboration of haunted stories based on true events.

The stories in this book are mostly hauntings that have happened around the world with numerous forms of haunted items or artifacts. Some are legends or stories and some are factual.

Please remember to leave a review after reading.

Follow Eve S. Evans on instagram: @eves.evansauthor or

@foreverhauntedpodcast

@theconsfearacypodcast

Or check out Eve's website to get up-to-date release information and limited time deals! www.getevebooks.com

Check out our Bone-Chilling Tales to keep you awake segment on youtube for more creepy, narrated haunted stories by Eve S Evans.

Let me know on Instagram that you wrote a review and I'll send you a free copy of one of my other books!

Check out Eve on a weekly basis on one of her many podcasting ventures. Forever Haunted, The Ghosts That Haunt Me with Eve Evans, or A Truly Haunted Podcast.

50 TERRIFYING REAL GHOST STORIES

From the creators of Forever Haunted Podcast

EVE S EVANS

1 The Basement

This took place right next to the asylum I was living in. The place was shut down for several reasons. Officially they said the building had fallen into disrepair. But among the residence there were claims of ghosts, unusual deaths and injuries from people who had been in there. At times even before we were sneaking over there, we had seen movement in the windows, leering faces, and other strange happenings that we couldn't explain.

This is one experience that happened to me at this place. It was me, Billy and Tammy going into this place. We went around the back side. Some of the floors had windows and some did not. In the back there was a window that had no glass in it. However, the window was high enough that we had to lift the others to the ledge. I was typically the last one up because I could jump the high enough to grab the hands of the others then they would pull me up. First thing is the entire area is gloomy. There is glass on the floor and debris all over the place. Other than that, it simply looks like a building that was old and falling further into disrepair.

The wind could be heard blowing through holes in the walls making strange noises. There is enough light in the building that we can see clearly. We went throughout the building looking around. The first floor has no windows except in the front which are slitted giving it a prison like feel to it. The three floors above had windows that let in the light so you could see bedframes, blankets, sheets, and curtains. The floor is stained brown and there are scorch marks here and there in the building. Some of the windows are intact, but most were not which let the wind blow through the building making the temperature fluctuate constantly as we walked through.

We found some of the windows that faced our dorm on the top floor where we had seen some movement. There were no curtains in the windows which could explain what we could have seen. On the floor there were several stains and scorch marks and a place where it looked like someone had bult a fire and had used some of the debris around the building to burn. Obviously there had been people in here at some point in time.

After we check out the top two floors and found nothing of note we went back down the stairs to a landing on the first floor and we see a room just light enough by the ambient light from the front of the building.

This is the first time we really were able to notice the smell. On the upper floors you would get a whiff of garbage every now and again, but the wind kept most of this to minimum. That was not the case here. The first thing we noticed was there was not as much air current in this room and the room smelled of rot and decay.

We headed down toward the light of the main door. It is locked and barred so of course we cannot get through. There are rooms on either side of the hall where the main door is located so we started looking into these doors. Most of these are rooms that have been made into a modified school. The first one we go into is a bathroom. The room looks like it has not seen some use in quite a while. Some of the toilets are broken and there is paper and rock all over the floor.

As we continue down the hall, we start to hear things that we had not been hearing before. We can hear mice scurrying around and objects being displaced. At 12 years old this only added to the disturbing feelings that this place elicited. There were also a lot more burn marks down here than there had been on the upper floors. It looked as if a fire had broken out in this part of the building at some point.

We continued looking into rooms for about 10 minutes and that is when we hear a door slam. We cannot determine if it came from in front or behind us. We freeze and try to listen for any clue as to where the noise came from. We listen for a few minutes and we begin to hear footsteps. They are not moving quickly but rather at a steady walk. As far as we knew we were alone in the building. At this point we wanted to know where the footsteps were coming from, but at the same time we wanted to leave. Bolstered by each other's company we decided to stay.

Taking cues from the sounds we heard, we followed the footsteps. They seemed sound to be going away from us. We picked up the pace as we give pursuit thinking one of the others was trying to scare us. We come across another staircase that was barricaded up with display cases and bedframes. We go down a hallway that opens into a big dorm that looks like it once could have been a library. The shelves are empty though. There is only one exit to the library so there is no way someone could have gotten in another way.

We go back and pass the blocked stairwell and go the opposite direction. We go through what appeared to be a cafeteria for the building. Be go back another hallway with classrooms and desks in the. There are no stairs around for someone to get away. We go back to the stairs where we came down from the second floor and realize there is not any place someone could have gone except downstairs to the basement. This is particularly scary because this is where most of the stories come from about scary things happening to people.

We notice a door that is off its hinges and the smell is extremely strong in this part of the building. We are talking to each other and we hear a thump in front of us. In the shadows we see movement, but we can't really catch what it was because our flashlights are pointed a different direction at the time.

We give chase thinking that we have caught the people trying to scare us. Ahead we hear bumps and thuds like someone is trying to get away. Our lights are pointing forward, but we do not see anything. We do not see anything moving ahead of us, but we hear the sound of running footsteps.

Ahead of us we see a door slam and hear footsteps. The problem is we do not see what closed the door. At this point fear gets the better of us and we start to run away as fast as we can go. It might have been my imagination, but it seemed as if the footsteps were chasing us now.

We ran back to the stairwell and up to the second floor. We continued to run to the room where we got into the building just in time to see another group trying to get in. After hearing our story, they decided it was better to leave with us. We ran all the way back to the dorm in a complete panic.

2 Gampa

Every family has some relative somewhere in their family tree that has some strange story associated with them. My family, well there have been several people who have claimed to be "sensitive" or just came right out and said that they could communicate with spirits. It has always been a touchy subject within our family because they were always labeled crazy cousin... or uncle so and so is a bit touched if you know what I mean. But for the most part these people were shunned by the majority and were essentially treated as if they did not exist. That is why this incident was so disturbing and heartbreaking at the same time.

My son Ian was only three years old when this happened. She seemed to be hanging on to her "Terrible Two's" a little longer than we had hoped. She would scream, cry and yell almost constantly, not because she wanted or needed anything but simply for attention. We tried everything we could to try and calm him down. I don't know how many books we read just to try and find a way for us to help him.

Then one day he was screaming at the top of his lungs for what seemed like a solid hour. He was getting horse it had been going on for so long. If someone could have heard him, I am sure they thought we were mistreating him in some way. Then he seemed to turn toward the hallway and suddenly stopped. He smiled and began to crawl to an open part of the room and sat there staring off into space. Every minute or so he would laugh, giggle, or say a few words to seemingly no one. It was odd and kind of creepy at the time, but it was a relief from his usual behavior.

I started to get worried when this continued for over an hour. I tried to pull him away but as soon as I tried he would go back to screaming until I let him go and he could crawl back to the place that he had been before.

Finally I just came out and asked him who he was talking to. "Ian, who are you talking to?"

"Nobody."

That is all I could get from him that first day. I thought that maybe he had developed some sort of imaginary friend or something. Lots of kids do that kind of thing so I did not worry about it too much at first. When it continued though past the first week, I decided that it would be best to talk to him about this "friend" of his. I wanted Ian to have friends in the real world and had been reaching out to some of the moms that I knew in order to give him some kids his own age to play with hoping that would stop the fantasy.

No matter what I did though he would just sit there and stare down into the hall talking to nobody. He would completely ignore the other kids almost like he had no interest in them at all. With no other options I decided to take him to a child psychologist to see if they could figure out what was going on with my son.

At first Ian seem reluctant to talk about his conversations that he was having continuing to say that he was talking to no one. But finally, after a couple of sessions, he finally admitted to who his invisible friend was.

"I'm talking to gampa."

This was an answer that I really did not expect. My father had died even before he was born and so he had never met him before. To this point I had never even heard him use that word before which was the strangest part of the answer he gave. To have a concept of who that was seemed beyond what my 3-year-old should have been capable of. When the psychologist asks Ian to describe what he looked like though what he said scared me. Somehow, he was able to give an accurate and detailed description of what my dad had looked like shortly before he died. Frankly, it seemed unbelievable.

After this session I really was at a loss for what to do. I mean was it possible that my dad was visiting Ian? I did not know what to think. Encouraging it seemed risky at best because I didn't want to feed the fantasy which I believed it to be, on the other hand though he wasn't hurting anyone and he hadn't been throwing the fits that he had for over a year now. Any improvement no matter the cause was a welcome change.

A week later I had my answer to whether it was real or not. I was asleep in my bed when the sound of my door shutting woke me up. I thought maybe Ian had come into my room and was looking to sleep with me that night, something that he did on occasion.

Turning and opening my eyes just a crack I noticed a soft blue glow coming from the end of my bed. Unsure of the cause I rolled over the rest of the way and for a split second I saw my father standing there looking down on me smiling. The feeling I got when I saw him can only be described as an overwhelming sense of love. It was like being warmed from the inside. It was so powerful that I started to cry.

For some reason my dad had come to comfort my son during a time in his life where he must have needed him a great deal. After I saw my dad in my room that night Ian no longer sat by himself and talked to my dad. Whatever purpose he meant to serve was done now. Ian also seemed to be cured of the "Terrible twos" as well. I am so happy that my son had the ability to meet his grandfather. As time goes on, I am sure that the memory of what happened will fade but I will always know that my dad loves his grandson.

3 Spiders

Me and my wife are getting advanced in our years, so when it comes to sleeping through the night it does not really happen. I am having to get up time and again to go to the bathroom. One of those crappy parts to look forward to when everyone gets older, I guess. Next to our bed we have a mirror that I catch my reflection out of the corner of my eye. Even though I know it is a mirror and I see it during the day, my shadowed reflection never fails to creep me out. I've considered asking my wife to move it, but I know it will sound like the ramblings of an old man beginning to lose his mind, so I haven't mentioned anything.

One evening I was really feeling worn out, so I told my wife I was going to go take a little nap before dinner. She told me she would get me up when it was getting close and went off somewhere else in the house. She told me that at some point she had to use the bathroom whose door faces our bed. She said that in the mirror in the bathroom she saw me sit up and start to crawl down to the end of our bed. Given that I am in my late 70's I don't have the strength or range of motion that I used to so when she saw me lift myself up off the bed with my legs and arms like some sort of bug she found it really strange.

She then saw me stand up, walk over and lean against the doorframe to the bathroom and just stand there. She has told me the look in my eyes was really unsettling. It was like I was a different person she would later describe. She turned to talk to me but when she looked where she had seen me in the mirror, I was still sound asleep in bed. Unease and bewilderment gave way to fear as she grappled with what she had just seen.

She said at this point she started to panic, not sure if she was having some sort of health crisis or something else was going on. She backed up against the sink and just stared at me in the bed. She was torn between wanting to let me sleep and waking me to set her mind at ease. As much as she did not want to be alone right then, she wanted to let me get some rest. When she turned around to look back in the mirror the entire thing had been covered in a thin coat of condensation and there were handprints all over the mirror like someone had touched it over and over again. That is when she screamed.

I sat quickly upright in bed unsure of what was going on. It took me a few seconds to get my bearings but when I did, I was at her side as quickly as I could. She pointed out the mirror too scared to say anything else just then and buried her head into my shoulder. I did not really know what she was so worried about since it just looked like she had touched the mirror while it was wet. When I asked her what was wrong she had calmed down long enough to tell me what she had seen in the mirror and then how the handprints seemed to have just appeared out of nowhere.

A cold chill ran down my spine, and it wasn't just from the story my wife had told. As fantastic as it sounded, she was not someone who would scare easily or to make up something like this. I myself already didn't like what I saw every night in the mirror next to our bed and this wasn't about to help matters either.

I felt a cold breeze pass along the back of my neck suddenly and the hair on the back of my neck started standing on end. I started looking around to see if there was anything in the room with us but all I saw was the empty room. My wife and I both turned toward the door as footsteps seemed to be walking away from the bathroom and into our bedroom. I could feel her begin to shiver in my arms and I knew she had heard them too. We both sat there for a few minutes not sure if we wanted to follow into our bedroom. The sounds had been scary enough to keep us frozen in place where we were.

Finally I decided I had stood there long enough and I walked back into where I had been soundly sleeping just a few minutes before. The room was warm and did not seem off to me. Even if it did though I am not sure I could have done anything about it anyways. Not wanting to be left alone she followed close behind me as we pushed deeper into the bedroom. No strange noises happened, no cold breezes, just stillness and silence. Whatever had been there seemed to have left.

Thankfully there has not been an encore performance to this event in our home. Frankly, I think I would move out of there if there was. Our home is older so I suppose that it is possible that someone had died there at one point in its history and could still be residing here with us. I have always been interested in the paranormal and spirits, but always from a distance and that is how I'd prefer it to.

4 Don't wake the baby

Our daughter was born in the fall. For the first little bit, we were living with my mom and dad until our house was finished being built.

Our room was upstairs and little Emma's room was to the right side of ours.

The first odd thing to happen was when my husband Richard and I were in bed talking about politics. (We are both big on that topic and loved to debate with each other.)

I heard Emma sigh while sleeping and it sounded like the monitor moved a little bit. It was hard to describe the sound. It was like the sound of when someone bumps a camera while its on a camera stand.

We both looked over at the monitor and saw what looked like two or maybe three shadow people standing at the foot of her bassinet.

Richard jumped out of bed and went to check on her while I was still staring at the baby cam.

The minute he flipped the lights on, they all disappeared. Like poof, gone. It blew my mind.

I yelled at him to shut the lights off again and he did. Nothing was on the monitor. Odd. Did we see what we thought we saw?

With nothing else happening on the monitor, we brushed it off as our mind playing tricks and went to sleep.

About a month later, in the middle of the night, we were fast asleep. We were jolted from our slumber to what sounded like fists banging on the other side of our wall (Emma's room).

Again, Richard jumped out of bed and ran in there while I hastily grabbed the baby cam and checked it. I saw nothing out of the ordinary. No shadows, nothing.

Richard came back in, shrugging. He hadn't seen anything unusual either.

Fast forward about three months or so. We were about two weeks away from our house being finished. It was the day we did the final walk-through on our home. My mom and dad had flown to Hawaii the day before to celebrate their wedding anniversary, so we had the house to ourselves for a whole week.

Like before, it was bedtime. Richard had already dozed off and was lightly snoring and my eyes were getting tired as well. I was just reaching for the lamp to shut it off when I heard what sounded like two jumps. It was like someone jumped two times in the hallway really hard.

I pulled my hand back and just laid there and listened. I wasn't sure if I'd really heard anything. I was really tired so maybe my mind was messing with me.

Suddenly, I heard footsteps. It was a pounding down the hall, like a sprint headed right for our side of the hallway. I punched Richard in the arm, and he awoke just as the footsteps sounded like they reached our door.

It took everything in me to not scream at the top of my lungs, I was so terrified. Something had just run full force from one end of the hallway to either our door or Emma's.

"What the hell?" Richard squealed. "Why did you punch me?"

"Did you hear it?" I hissed a whisper.

"Hear what?"

"Footsteps. Something ran from the other side of the hall and stopped when it reached our door. Please go check." I gave him a terrified glance.

He sighed and shook his head as he got out of bed and went out into the hallway. Then I heard him open Emma's door and check her room. Nothing.

By the time our house was ready to move into, we were both sleep deprived and eager to get the heck out of my parent's home.

After we moved in, I feared maybe something could have followed us there. We've been in our new home for four years now with nothing otherworldly happening.

5 Must say goodbye

I was thirteen when it began. I was elated to attend a sleepover for a friend's birthday. I was fairly new to this school, so it was a big deal that I fit in.

After all the party activities and movies, we were upstairs in my friend Lilianna's room. Some of us were getting sleepy, others were still wide awake and chatty.

Lillianna pulled a Ouija board out from underneath her bed and started giggling. She asked if we wanted to play. Everyone but me immediately agreed.

Most of the girls did not believe in such things but growing up watching ghost movies I was more hesitant.

With all their curious gazes cast my direction awaiting my answer I nodded and agreed. I just didn't want to be teased for being the only one who didn't want to play with it. That was probably my biggest mistake.

The girls sat in a circle and we put the board on the floor in the middle of us. We all leaned over and put a finger on the planchette.

Hailey began by asking the questions. First it was simple things like, "Hello," or "How are you," or "When did you die." None of these brought much of an answer. Everyone but I was beginning to get discouraged. I was elated and ready to stop playing this game.

Sophie asked a question next. "Would you like to hurt one of us?"

We all looked at her in disbelief. Why the heck would you ask a spirit board something so insane. If there was something there it would take that as an invitation!

The planchette finally did move to our horror and spelled out my name. Nichole. I jerked my finger off the planchette as if I had been burned and refused to partake in anything else.

There was the usual arguing of, "You made it move," – "No you did," – "That's not funny."

I sat off in the corner of the room trying to gain my wits while they disagreed between themselves. I was ready for this slumber party to be over at this point. I just wanted to go home.

Mostly I was embarrassed that I let it phase me so much because it probably wasn't real anyways. However, part of me felt uneasy that it had pinpointed me. Maybe it *was* just one of the girls trying to mess with me.

Hailey came over to me and gave me a big sympathetic hug. "I'll put the board away and we can do something else. We can watch another movie and I will let you pick it."

I nodded and watched as she stuffed the board back under her bed. Then I sunk deep in my sleeping bag and tried my best to push the game from my mind so I could sleep.

Around two in the morning I awoke to wetness on my face. It was warm and syrupy. I sat upright in my sleeping bag and wiped at my face. It was blood.

Looking around the room I noticed all of the girls were awake, but Aimee and they were staring at me in panic. Confused, I ran to the bathroom and took care of my bloody nose.

Once I got it under control, I came back in the bedroom to all eyes again on me. "What?!" I demanded.

Hailey gulped, "You were talking in your sleep."

"Like a lot," Sophie chimed in.

"What did I say?" I asked as I situated back into my sleeping bag while holding toilet paper to my nose.

"Couldn't understand most of it honestly," Hailey stated.

"You did say 'Die' before you woke up though," Sophie recalled.

"You guys are nerds. You are freaking yourselves out. Go to sleep." I was trying to keep my cool. Acting tough and unphased by all of it. But to be honest I felt a little uneasy, and not quite myself. Also, I never got nose bleeds. I think I may have had one in my entire life. Weird.

The next morning, I was relieved to finally be home and far away from that board it gave me the creeps.

I took a long shower and laid on my bed reading a book I had started over a week ago. And then there was a loud bang on my bedroom door. Like one loud knock. I went over to the door and opened it. No one was there and nothing was on the carpet.

I shut the door and walked back over to the bed. Before I could lay back down on the bed, I felt it again. Hot, sticky and warm. My nose was bleeding again.

I rushed to the bathroom and took care of it. Why was I having all of these nose bleeds all of the sudden? Stress maybe?

I tried my best to ignore it. I laid back down and held the tissue to my nose with one hand and my book in the other and tried to clear my mind.

I thought that as long as I didn't believe in it, or acknowledge it was weird it couldn't happen. But that's not true now, is it?

The rest of the day was fine and nothing unusual happened. I was beginning to be my bright and cheery self again by bedtime. I was miles from that board, and it couldn't phase me.

At bedtime I turned my tv volume on low as just some slight background noise to keep my mind from wandering to anything negative. I drifted off fairly easily and slept soundly.

At three in the morning I awoke with a startle. I was not in my bed. I squinted my eyes in the darkness and looked around to figure out where I was.

I was in the kitchen, standing in front of the island. I looked down at my hand and I was holding a knife. Immediately I placed it on the counter. That's when I saw the word *die* spelled out in salt on the countertop. What the heck was happening?

I wanted to run upstairs and wake up my parents I was so terrified. But they would think I was making it up or being ridiculous. I swallowed my fear and wiped the salt off into the trash. I would find answers myself.

I ran up the stairs two at a time in fear something was following me. I seriously felt like I was being watched, it was creepy.

In my room I pulled out my laptop and searched multiple articles on Ouija boards. That's when my heart sank. We never said "goodbye" when we were playing with the board. We needed to say goodbye and maybe all of this would stop.

The next morning, I called Hailey and asked if I could come over so that we could say goodbye on the board. She agreed and we did just that.

After we said goodbye, I have not had any more sleepwalking issues or seen the word die written anywhere. I still get chronic nose bleeds however, and the doctors cannot figure out why.

6 The depths of evil

I had a more fortunate childhood than most. I grew up in a house that was quite large in size, surrounded by wineries and mountains. On the outside, the house was aged but serene. A historic gem tucked neatly in between a vast forest and acres of aromatic grapes.

I distinctively remember when I would play in the backyard how the aroma of grapes would surround me like a heavenly embrace. I miss that smell. However, I do not miss that house.

The home was built in the late 1800s. The outside had weathered well over the years, but the inside needed constant repair. I remember how my mother would get frustrated every few months over something breaking. Whether it be the stove not working, the pipes needing mending, or floorboards creaking, it seemed like a pit hole of endless restorations.

Due to the house's age, at first, we easily brushed things off as the house settling. There would be knocks, creaks, bangs; you name it. My parents would say, "This is just an old house. It's just settling. No need to fret."

Like an obedient child, I believed them... at first. Then the disembodied voices began. First, in the cellar, when I was fetching a bottle of wine for my parents. My mom was making dinner, and my father was changing out of his work clothes. My mom had turned to me, soup ladle in hand, and said, "Johnny, can you fetch Mommy a bottle of the Rose label wine?"

I'd glanced at her then at the cellar door. I hated the cellar. It just emitted the creepiest of vibes. I mean, truly, what little kid enjoys going down in a dark half-finished basement anyways? None that I can think of.

Knowing that her question was more of a statement than a question, I nodded hesitantly and made my way to the cellar door. The steps creaked under my feet as my eyes searched the pitch black for the light. It was one of those pull string lights, and of course, it resided at the bottom of the stairs, which was completely unhelpful.

As I neared the bottom of the stairs, I heard shuffling. Like you would hear if you were dragging something across a concrete floor. I stopped in place and listened, my heart beating faster with every passing second. I heard nothing more. I shrugged to myself and begged myself to believe it must have just been my footsteps on the stairs. I continued to the light.

Once I lifted my hand to wave into the darkness to find the string to the light, I froze. Disembodied voices were coming from my right. The only thing to my right, however, was a furnace and an entry to a small room no one ever used.

I could not make out what any of the whispers were saying, but I knew they were indeed voices. Were they voices of the dead? I trembled, turned on my feet, and started running up the stairs praying to God I would not fall and break my neck.

I burst out of the cellar door breathless, and my mom, still stirring dinner, looked up from the pot, surprised.

"Johnny, why are you running around in the cellar? You are causing such a racket!" she scolded me, waving her ladle in the air before she went back to stirring. "Did you fetch the bottle?"

I was not going back down there, so I lied. "The light bulb is burnt out, and I can't find my way around."

Just as the words came out of my mouth, my father came sauntering into the room. "I'll have a look at it, Honey," he leaned over and pecked her cheek and gave me a stern look as if punishing me with his eyes for my silliness of the dark.

He pushed past me and headed for the cellar. I turned my body and followed him with my eyes until he disappeared through the threshold. My mind was frantic with thoughts. Mostly worried my dad would not return.

After a minute, my father reappeared with a bottle in hand and handed it to my mother.

"What was wrong with the light?" My mom asked.

My father shot me a distasteful look, then softened himself as he turned to my mother, "Nothing, Honey, it just must have been too hard for Johnny to pull."

I eyed my feet in embarrassment and retreated to my room until dinner was ready.

I did not like being in the house by myself. If I would come home from school on any day and no one was home, I would wait in the front yard until someone else arrived home.

Why was this, you ask? Obviously, it was not just because of a silly cellar incident. No, no. Many more incidents happened throughout the years I cannot even count them all, let alone recollect them all.

I was terrified to be home alone because something was in that house. Probably multiple somethings rather. One liked my sister's bedroom. Who knows, maybe at one point in history, it was *their* room. No one knows for sure.

Getting back to my story, I will tell you about what I saw one day while waiting outside after school. As I'd mentioned, I refused to wait inside until someone else was home. My gut just told me not to risk it.

I was walking back and forth, pacing the long dirt driveway, and I felt like something was watching me. My first thought was possibly the trees, maybe a bird. I searched the tree line, then scanned up the trunks to the branches. There were so many trees that I shrugged it off and continued kicking dirt on the driveway, patiently passing the time.

Overwhelmed with another wave of uneasiness, I again looked around me. It felt like whatever it was, it was boring holes in me with its eyes, and I shuddered at the thought.

I turned to face the front of the house and combed the windows with my gaze. My eye fell upon my sister's window and the slightly parted blinds. I blinked multiple times and squinted at the window. Was I really seeing this? Did she have something propped against her window that may have laid against the blinds, causing them to part like that?

I thought long and hard and shook my head at my own inner question. Her bed was next to the window. There would be nothing but the side of it against that wall.

My eyes grew wider as I continued to stare up at the window in shock. I watched on as the blinds slowly retreated and fell back into place. I gulped. Just at that moment, my sister bumped into me. "Last one to the house is a rotten egg!" She giggled as she sprinted towards the front door.

I was the competitive type, but not that day. That day I would let her win. I was not going inside that house until my parents got home; however long that took, I would wait.

As I have made you aware, this house of haunts has many stories and evil memories. There is one last one I feel like I should share that will help you understand why I say something resided in my sister's room. Sure, the window event was creepy in itself, but this one, this one takes the cake.

First of all, there was the feeling. Whenever I went into my sister's room, I was just overwhelmed by a feeling of "invading" as if it was silently telling me to "get out". I brushed it off, of course, because at that time, we hadn't lived there long, and I just assumed it was the age of the house leaving me unsettled.

Then one evening, I was in my sister's room watching television with her while our mom made dinner. As I have explained, her bed is against the wall with the window. Well, her dresser was perched over by her bedroom door near the hallway. We were laughing at a silly kid's show. The sun was going down outside, but the room was still quite lit with daylight. Enough so that I was able to get over the creepy feeling I would get being in her room.

As a commercial break came on, I got up to go to the bathroom. As I stood, everything atop of her dresser, a hairbrush, a few articles of clothing, and her makeup bag fell off onto the floor.

Unable to take a step forward, I glanced over my shoulder at my sister to see if she had seen that happen as well. The look on her face was priceless. Her mouth was agape in a way I had never seen, her eyes beamed as wide as they would go, and she was nibbling her bottom lip. She brought her wide eyes from the dresser and met mine. Yes, indeed, she had seen it too.

Now sometimes in this house, I was scared, and sometimes I liked to tease whatever it was just to see what it would do. So, on my way to the bathroom, before I exited her room, I asked it to put everything back the way it was before I came back. My sister rushed to my side, refusing to be alone in the room, and waited outside the bathroom for me to finish.

Once we were back in her room, everything that had been brushed off on her floor was back atop her dresser. Now that was some trick. It took my sister nearly a week to agree to sleep in her room again after that one.

My room was on the opposite side of the wall to my sister's. I would hear scratching noises in the middle of the night, like there was possibly a rat in the wall. I'd chalk it up to just that because the house was historically old and, as I mentioned, needing constant repairs.

One evening the scratching was so loud I thought something was going to break through the wall at any moment. I was tossing and turning in bed, even tried a pillow over my head to muffle the noise to no avail.

Defeated, I went to her room to investigate the noise. I wondered how she could sleep through it! As I entered her dark room, the noise halted. I held my breath, and the feeling of not being wanted was the heaviest it had ever been. It was as if in my mind's eye, I could see it glaring at me through the darkness of the room, daring me to take one more step forward.

I stood there in a panic. I was not going to walk any further in the room, but I did not feel safe turning my back to the darkness to walk out of it either. With a quivering whisper, I spoke to the darkness, "I'm just going back to bed. I'll leave you alone."

As I began to turn around, something quite solid knocked into my legs and took me down. My legs buckled, and I landed with a crumpled thud on her floor.

My first reaction was to search the darkness for what had knocked me off my feet. I thought ghosts were opaque? How could they hit you with such a solid force? I have never answered that question. But something had, in fact, hit me so hard it took me down.

I remained on the floor for a good few minutes, wondering if my sister had woken from the noise, but eventually, her soft snores permeated the blackness, and I knew somehow she slept right through it.

After finally gaining my wits, I climbed to my feet ever so slowly. This time I was going to walk backwards towards the hallway until I was fully out of her room then be-line it for my room. That was the plan anyway until the scratching noise resumed right next to where I stood. Then all my planning went to the wind, and my feet took flight. I ran so fast out of her room; I almost couldn't stop before I hit the wall. I turned and ran to my room and shut my door, and locked it.

The scratching noise continued all night, unlike other nights when it would come and go. But I will tell you one thing; I never investigated the sound again after that night. I had my mom buy me some earplugs and started using them on a nightly basis.

Did I ever see anything in the house? Many times. Mostly out of the corner of my eye. But the experiences seemed to be creepier, not knowing exactly what or who was causing it.

We lived in that house for fifteen years. My sister and I dubbed it the house of horrors. I'm still not quite sure what was causing the activity, but the

house had been built over battlefields,
that much I know.

7 The Locket

A couple of years ago, some friends and I were going on a rafting trip together. We always tried to get together to do something every year since we all graduated from college and moved to different parts of the country. This just happened to be the activity we could all agree on this year. The trip itself was really fun, and it was nice to see all of my old friends, but this isn't a story about outdoor adventures.

When we got out of the river, I happened to look down on the ground and saw a glint from something buried in the sand. I reached down, curious about what it could be. I was really surprised to see that a small silver locket came out with a chain attached to it. It was oval in shape but didn't have any sort of markings on it that made it distinguishable from any other locket of its type. Curious, I opened it to see what could have been inside of it, but when I opened it, there wasn't anything on either side, just blank spots where pictures could be placed.

At this point, my silence had been noticed, and my friend Julie saw what I had in my hand. After finding out that I had just found it in the sand, she seemed to take an interest in it, and I gave it to her since I really had no interest in it other than thinking it was cool. After a picnic lunch, we all separated. Everything after this is what Julie told me happened to her after she got home.

At first, she told me nothing was out of the ordinary. In fact, she didn't unpack her bag for a couple of days. When she did so, she found the locket inside the pocket of the jeans she had been wearing when we went rafting. At first, she didn't really remember why she had been drawn to it so strongly at the time. After all, it was just a simple oval locket, nothing special. She put it in her jewelry box and put it out of her mind.

Julie is typically a night owl, but she told me that for the first few days of her getting back from her trip that she constantly felt tired. No matter how much sleep she got the night before, it was like she woke up exhausted. She was going to go to the doctor if she continued to feel poorly the next day just to make sure.

On the fourth day back, she woke up like she always did. This time though, she seemed to feel fully rested. Julie convinced herself almost immediately that she must have caught a minor cold during the time she was away, and it had taken a few days for her to kick it. She went into the bathroom to brush her teeth when she looked in the mirror and noticed that she was wearing the silver locket. She knew that she hadn't put it on or even taken it out of her jewelry box since the day she had put it there. She told me she was weirded out big time. She had never been known to sleepwalk, but even if she had done that, to have walked over to the box and picked out this one item in a dead sleep didn't seem right or even possible.

Without any other real explanation, she just had to accept either she had put it on and forgotten or had somehow been able to put it on herself while she was asleep. She took it off and put it back, and finished getting ready for work. That night when she got home, she was sorting through the mail that she had gotten that day, mostly junk mail, and she happened to look over to the end of the counter. There, on the end, sat the locket. The hair on the back of her neck stood on end. For the first time, she said that she thought someone was in her apartment and had been there since the night before.

Julie grabbed a knife from the butcher block and started going from room to room, looking for signs that someone was there. The thing that she said didn't make sense to her, though, is why put the locket out? Why would someone not steal the jewelry, her laptop, the television? Why just put it out on the counter or put it on her while she slept? What kind of weirdo was she dealing with? After a thorough search of the house, she determined that no one else was there, but it was possible they had left while she was at work. She called a 24-hour locksmith and had them come out and rekey the locks to her place just to make sure she felt safe.

That night she went to bed a little nervous, but after a long day at work and the anxiety she felt when she came home, she quickly fell asleep wrapped in the warmth of her blankets. Sometime in the middle of the night, she woke up feeling cold; the blankets that had been there were no longer on her. When she looked around the bed, she didn't see them anywhere. If she kicked them off, they would have been on the sides or the foot of the bed, but the floor was empty. Julie told me she felt like her home, the place where she was supposed to be safe, no longer felt that way. 'Violated' was the word she used.

The thing that seemed to scare her the most, though, was that the locket was back around her neck when she woke up. Terrified of what it meant, she ripped it off and threw it across the room. As soon as she did so, an intense feeling of nausea passed over her. She told me she thought she was going to throw up and got up and tried to race to the bathroom. When she was a few feet from the door, though, it slammed shut, and she ran straight into the door.

This is where her story gets stranger, though. Julie told me she would have fallen to the ground, but some unseen force seemed to pin her to the wall. She couldn't move, no matter how hard she fought. This seemed to last for about fifteen seconds before she slumped to the floor. She said she knew she had to get out of there as quickly as she could. She knew that it wasn't a person doing these things to her but some sort of ghost. She packed a quick overnight bag and checked into a hotel for the night, just trying to get some distance between her and whoever was back there.

The next day she went back thinking that the daylight would protect her from what was happening there. When she walked in, she noticed that the blankets and sheets that had been on her bed were sitting on one of the chairs in her living room. She hadn't gotten more than ten steps in when she heard something hit the floor in the kitchen. Walking over, she was sure she knew what it was before she even saw it. There on the tiles was the silver locket. Ever since she had brought it home, there had been problems. Whatever was in her apartment, this thing was attached to this piece of jewelry.

She ended up taking the locket to a second-hand store and leaving it in the overnight donation drop area. She hoped that by removing it from her home that she would also remove the presence that had been there. Nothing happened after she got rid of the locket, but a few months later, she ended up moving out and finding somewhere else to live. I think that she never really felt safe in there after that. I can't say that I blame her. In her position, I would have done the same.

8 Trick but no trick

When I was younger, my group of friends and I used to go trick or treating together every Halloween. We have known each other since before kindergarten, so we have been doing this for quite some time. Our parents had always gone with us until we were eleven when we were finally able to convince them to let us go out by ourselves with the promise that we would only go to houses in the neighborhood. We readily agreed, just excited to be getting to go out on our own.

That year we were all going as our favorite superheroes. Me, I chose

Superman. I was all dressed up, and my friends were there, and we were ready to go out and have fun. My mom gave all of us the stereotypical talk about not talking to strangers, which got a collective eye roll from the entire group, but there wasn't any way she was going to let any of us out of the house without it. Safety speech over, we walked out the door, ready to score a bunch of candy.

It had been about an hour, and we weren't yet ready to call it a night. We still had a lot of houses that we could go to so we could increase our stash, so we walked over to the next block. We had just started walking away from the first house when we all saw a little kid in a ghost outfit, just a long sheet with some eye holes cut out of it, standing there with a pumpkin bucket at the end of the path. They looked by their size to be about six or seven years old, so definitely too young to be out on their own, but there wasn't anyone around that seemed to be with them. I was a little concerned that they were lost, so I went up to talk to them.

"Hey, where are your parents? Are you all alone?" All I could see was a set of bright blue eyes staring back at me, almost terrified to see me.

I figured that the kid was shy and that he was told not to talk to strangers. I tried to ask for a name and introduced myself and my friends, but all I got was silence. This kid was either terrified of us or completely mute, being dressed as Superman, and all, I wasn't going to just leave the kid there by himself, so I took his hand and tried to lead him with me. When I grabbed the hand through the sheet, it felt really cold, which seemed odd at the time since it was pretty warm for this time of year.

We walked down the block. I did everything I could to get the little ghost to talk, but they remained silent. Every time we would go up to the door to a house, the kid would refuse to move an inch down the walkway to get candy. Their bucket didn't have a single piece of candy in it, which seemed sad; I mean, why go trick or treating if you weren't going to go get any candy? But the more I thought about it, the more it seemed to make sense; this kid was out here all by themself and wouldn't even talk to another kid, not to mention trying to get them to go up to the door of a complete stranger.

As the night was coming to a close, I was unsure what to do about our silent new friend. We hadn't seen anyone out looking for a lost kid, and it wasn't like he didn't stand out given the low-tech costume they had on. Once we had gone to the last house, we planned on hitting; I made a decision. I would take him back to my house and tell my mom what was going on. It wasn't like she could be too mad at me since it wasn't like I was bringing some stray dog home. I mean, this was a lost kid. I had to do it. Not wanting the kid to go home empty-handed, I convinced my friends to each give up some of their candy so the kid could have some treats for later. Not everyone was happy about it since they had done all the work to get the candy, and now they were giving it up, but in the end, they all relented and picked out a number of choice pieces out of their pillowcases.

It is a tradition that we leave the kid's house that we start out at until last, thinking that we will be able to split up all the remaining candy that is left unclaimed at the end of the night. So, we walk up to the door of my home, ready to give my mom our best, "Trick or Treat?" that we can. I want the ghost to at least have a chance to go to one house, so I grab the little kid's hand, and we walk up the steps to my front door. I ask the ghost if they want to press the doorbell, but all I get is a slight shake of the head telling me no. Not wanting to wait any longer, one of my friends steps up and presses the button.

My mom comes to the door with a big bowl of candy, ready to start dishing it out to my friends and me, but then she gets this weird look on her face when she sees me. I don't really know why she is looking at me so weird.

"What are you doing, dragging that sheet around with you?" She cocks her head to the side.

I didn't know what she was talking about, I mean, it wasn't the greatest costume, but the kid was obviously young. I had some pretty silly costumes growing up myself. I told her we had found this kid standing by themself on the sidewalk, and we didn't want to leave them there.

"So, you took their ghost costume and ran off with it? Why would you do that?" She looked like she was about to get angry.

I turned to look at the kid, but all I had in my hand was a sheet. The pumpkin bucket was sitting neatly on the ground like it had been placed there so it wouldn't tip over, and the sheet lay in a pile on the ground with me holding one corner of it. I started to stutter and stammer, not sure what to say. I mean, I had just been holding the kid's hand just a few seconds ago. There was no way they could have gotten away without us noticing. But here I stood with a sheet and a pumpkin bucket. The kid had disappeared.

Now I don't know if for sure if that was a ghost that went trick or treating with us. Between the cold hand and the not speaking, I am led to believe that we had experienced an apparition of a kid. I know I was glad my friends had been there to back up my story even though my mom didn't seem to believe a word of it. That was definitely the craziest Halloween any of us ever had and one I won't forget.

9 Knock knock

Ever since I have moved into my home, I have been terrorized by something that seems to be getting closer and closer to me. At this point, I don't know what to do because I fear if it goes on any longer, then I might be in real danger. I guess I'll start at the beginning, and hopefully, someone can give me some sort of insight into what I can do.

The company I have worked at for the past ten years needed to transfer me to a city in Nebraska to help set up a new satellite office that we were opening in the Midwest. Because this was going to be a long-term assignment, the company offered to pay for my moving expenses. Really, what I was being told was that I would either be moving, or they would find someone who would. So, I went online and found a home in the area that I would be working in that I could get a long-term lease. It took me a few weeks, but I found a nice three-bedroom, two-bathroom home less than a mile from my office. A few weeks later, I was moving in and ready to start my new adventure.

The first day basically, all I got accomplished was getting boxes into the basic rooms that they were going into. My mattress was placed on the floor since I didn't have the energy left to put it together, and by this time, I was ready to go to sleep. I laid a couple of sheets down and grabbed a blanket from one of the boxes, and when I laid down, I was asleep almost immediately.

Sometime in the middle of the night, I woke up suddenly. I am usually a pretty deep sleeper, so this was an unusual thing for me. I looked around at first unsure of where I was from the strange shadowed shapes around me. Quickly though, I came to my senses and remembered that I was in my new place and that the weird shapes were just the unpacked boxes around me. I rolled back over, intending to go back to sleep, when I heard a strange rapping coming from somewhere in the front of the house. At first, I chalked it up to being unfamiliar noises from a strange new house and tried to ignore it. The longer it went on, though, I knew I wouldn't get back to sleep until I found out what was making the noise so I could quiet it or, if anything, quiet my imagination.

I got up and wrapped my robe around me, and walked out of my room. In my head, I just knew that as soon as I got to the living room where the noise seemed to be originating from, that it would cease. However, as soon as I breached the threshold, the knocking didn't stop; it continued on and on. It seemed to be coming from the window next to the door. This particular window was frosted, so I couldn't see out of it, but it appeared like there was some sort of figure standing out there. The door had a peephole, which I went up to and looked out of, but the step was surprisingly empty.

"Hello? Is someone there?" I asked out the door, but the only response that I got was the continued knocking sound.

At this point, I was fed up with the noise and decided to be brave and open the door. I tried to unlatch the deadbolt as quietly as I could, but when it disengaged, it made a hollow thunk that was probably quieter than I heard. I grabbed the handle with a shaking hand and took a deep breath, not sure of what I would confront on the other side. I twisted the handle and swung the door open as fast as I could. I could feel my pulse beating through my entire body, ready to run at a moment's notice, but when I looked out, there wasn't anyone there. The stoop was empty, and the knocking stopped.

I stepped back to look through the window again, and where the figure had been just seconds before seemed clear. I didn't understand how someone could have moved that fast. Maybe when they heard me undo the lock, they simply bolted, but the knocking had continued until I opened the door. There was no screen door, so it couldn't have been a breeze causing the noise, and there weren't any sort of decorations on the door that could have made the noise. All I could do was shake my head and close the door, thinking that maybe it had been some sort of bird or another nocturnal animal being mischievous.

I closed the door and relocked it, half expecting that the noise would start as soon as the bolt slid home, but no knocking came from the doorway. I walked back toward my room and stopped to take another look back at the door, almost daring the knocking to start again, but after it remained quiet for a few seconds, I walked back the rest of the way to my room, and after tossing and turning for a few minutes trying to silence my mind, I fell back asleep.

Nothing happened for a few days after that. I expected to hear the noise every night, but four nights passed before it seemed to return again. This time though, the noise sounded different than it had the first time. It seemed to echo throughout the house instead of just being centered at one point. As I got up to try and find the source, something about my home seemed to feel off, almost unwelcoming. I knew that the noise had unnerved me the first night, putting me on edge, but after a few nights of silence, I thought that things were going to be okay. That feeling of security seemed to fall away as if it had never been there as I walked towards the living room.

When I entered the room, I hugged my robe a little closer to me. The room felt colder than the rest of the house, and the unwelcome feeling seemed to ratchet up to another level. Every part of me told me to get out of there, to leave and go back to my room and get into bed, but I was a grown woman. I wasn't going to let a childish fear get the better of me. The knocking noise was louder tonight than it had been the other day. It took only a second to realize, though, why it was different; the noise wasn't coming from outside the door but inside of my house, in the coat closet a few feet inside the door.

A cold chill ran down my spine, and goosebumps sprang up on my arms. Someone or something was inside my house. The knocking had definitely put me on edge, and my mind ran to worst-case scenarios as I imagined someone had gotten in, and now they were trying to torment me by messing with my mind. As scared as I was, there was no way someone was going to come into the place I lived and do this kind of thing to me. In an act of stupidity, I walked over to the closet door and opened it up, ready for some knife-wielding psychopath to be there waiting for me. Just like the first time, though, as soon as I opened the door, the noise stopped, and I was left there staring into an empty closet.

Finding no one there had two effects, one, a wave of relief washed over me, knowing that someone wasn't waiting in my home trying to scare me. But mostly, it pissed me off. I knew I hadn't imagined the entire thing; at least I didn't think so. I had the place inspected before I moved in, and there hadn't been any sign of rodents of any kind in the walls, but who had heard of mice or rats making knocking noises? I know I hadn't. What else could it be, though? I decided I would call someone else to come and check the next day since obviously, the last guy didn't know what he was doing if he missed something so obvious. Feeling better about figuring out what was going on in my house, I walked back to my room. I had just gotten settled in bed when the knocking noise started again. I tried to ignore it, but I couldn't tune it out no matter what I did. That exterminator couldn't get here fast enough.

The next morning, I looked online for a company that had good reviews and would be willing to come out that day to check out my problem. I knew that same-day service was likely to cost me more money, but I wasn't going to go another night without sleep. It took me a couple of tries, but I finally got someone to agree to come and check out the house later that afternoon. When the guy arrived, I told him what had been going on, and he went to work looking for any sign of rats, mice, or some other vermin that were living in the walls. The idea that some dirty creature was inside my home made my skin crawl, and I was anxious to get rid of them. Three hours later, he came to the front door with a frown on his face. He told me that there wasn't any sign of any animals living inside of my house. I told him that couldn't be true, but he insisted that it was and handed me my invoice before walking back to his truck.

Now that I had two people telling me that there weren't mice in my walls and I hadn't found anything the two times that I had tried to confront whatever it was that was knocking in my home, I figured I should look online to see what else could be causing the knocking noises. I fired up the internet browser on my computer and went to a search engine, and typed in the words "Strange Knocking Noises Inside My Home". I noticed there were thousands of hits for the search, I didn't figure it would be such a popular subject, but that meant I was bound to find something that could help me.

The first thing on the list was a site dedicated to talking about haunted houses. I quickly passed by that because I didn't believe in ghosts, so I didn't take that option seriously. But the more I kept scrolling down, it seemed like nearly every page kept talking about ghosts, spirits, or demons of some kind. There were a lot of people with overactive imaginations, I guess. After a few pages of the same stuff, I shut down the internet. That's the problem with the internet these days; anyone can post anything, even if it is totally fake. I just hoped that I was done hearing noises, it could just be the house settling, that kind of made sense, but I really didn't believe that.

I didn't get any days off from the night time disturbance this time. It came back that night louder than ever. It sounded like someone was taking a hammer to the wall of my house. I got up to put an end to this once and for all; this couldn't go on indefinitely, I couldn't go on without getting any sleep. I walked down the hall, and I noticed why it seemed like it was so loud. The knocking noise had moved from the closet and now was going on inside the wall at the end of the hall where my bedroom was. In just four days, it had moved nearly half the distance from the front door to my bedroom. I took a few steps backward, trying to put distance between myself and this noise. Deep inside of me, a voice told me I was in danger, and I had to get out of there, but I stood there frozen, unable to come to grips with what was happening. I could see my breath, and I felt the cold air prickle my skin.

"What is happening in this house?" I asked to no one in particular.

I ran back to my room and shut the door, hoping that the barrier would give me some sense of safety, but all it did was make me feel trapped inside my own house. I pulled out my phone, and as much as I didn't want to consider the possibility that whatever was going on could be a ghost, I went to the internet and started to look over some of the pages talking about how you could tell if your house was haunted. At first, I felt stupid for even looking at these pages, but with every one, it seemed like the things that were happening pointed to this possibility.

The sites talked about knocking noises, feelings of dread, cold temperatures, and a variety of other things. What they didn't agree on was what to do to get rid of them. There were a few common things, though, which talked about burning jasmine to clean the home, crystals, or bringing in a medium to communicate with the deceased. There was only so much I was willing to try, but burning jasmine and maybe a crystal wasn't something I was opposed to trying. At least now I had a plan; as absurd as I thought it was, it was a plan.

Since I knew I was unlikely to be able to go to sleep, I looked up places where I could find crystals and jasmine. There were a few places but none that were really close by, the nearest being about fifty miles away. I didn't really think that I had much choice, though, and just accepted the fact that I would make the drive. The rest of the night, the sound would start and stop at various times and would last for two to ten minutes at a time. I tried to keep my mind occupied by reading, listening to music, or watching television, but my thoughts kept drifting to thoughts of ghosts and all the horror films I had watched about people being tormented by spirits. I had always just brushed this off as fantasy but confronting it now; they took on a whole new meaning.

I almost turned around a half dozen times the entire drive there as my logical mind grappled with what I thought was going on. You don't go over forty years of believing one thing and just overnight give it up without a fight. The only thing that kept me from doing so was not wanting to spend another sleepless night in that house. Finally, I pulled up in front of a small shop located in the corner of a strip mall.

Walking in, I could smell incense in the air and I saw an older woman that had wavy brown hair with streaks of grey going through it behind a counter. I had gotten there only about ten minutes after they had opened, so I was the only other person in the shop. I walked up to her, and she asked me if she could help me find anything. I must have looked a little skeptical because she seemed to sense my hesitation in telling her.

"Ah, I see I have a skeptic in my shop, huh?" Her smile and willingness to talk about exactly what I was thinking put me instantly at ease. "Well, how about this? Why don't you tell me why you are here?"

I proceeded to tell her everything that had happened since I had moved into the house. She sat there with the same kind smile the entire time as I told my story, never interrupting me once or making a face like she didn't believe a word I had said. Just a week ago, if someone had come to me with this type of story, I would have called them crazy. When I was done, she nodded to me and led me over to a section of shelves that held some dried bundles of plants. She took a small bundle and handed it to me.

"This is jasmine. You will want to burn it and make sure the smoke gets into every corner of all the rooms in your house."

Then we walked over to another set of shelves, and she told me that these crystals were quartz. They were all clear and came in various sizes and shapes. I waited for her to pick one out and hand it to me, but she just sat there and waited expectantly.

When I didn't make a move to take one, she went on further. "You have to be the one to pick the crystal; what one speaks to me may not speak to you."

I didn't know what she meant by the crystal had to speak to me, but I picked up a medium sized one, and we walked over to the register where I paid for my do-it-yourself ghostbuster kit and left. All things considered, this was a much better experience than I expected it to be. I don't know what I expected, but a kindly woman just looking to help wasn't it.

As soon as I got home, I took out my crystal and put it next to my bed. If this thing were going to protect me, I wanted it as close to me as possible when I was sleeping. I also took the jasmine, and after lighting, I went around to every room in my home and let the smoke fill the area for a few seconds before moving on to the next space. After I was done, the house didn't feel any different, but only time would tell if the cleansing had worked.

The next few days were quiet. I was convinced that the purification had worked, or most likely, that the noises had some sort of rational explanation and that whatever was causing them had worked itself out. Work was stressful, but after being able to sleep for the first time in a few days, I was able to actually get something accomplished. Then tonight came, and I am at a loss for what to do.

I went to bed at my regular time; with work so crazy the last few days, I didn't have the energy to stay up late even with a day off tomorrow. I quickly fell asleep after reading only a few pages of my latest novel. Around 2:00 am, I woke up to a pounding noise on my bedroom door. I bolted upright in bed and just sat there, unsure of what or who could be on the other side. I didn't dare open the door. Obviously, if someone was there, they didn't need my help getting in, and if it was a ghost, the cleansing had obviously failed to get rid of it. With the force of the pounding on the door, whatever it was, it seemed angry.

So, I sat there, unsure of what to do. Am I being stalked by something evil? Does it just want to say hello and let me know that it is present, does it think that I am intruding on its home, or does it have some other nefarious intentions towards me? I know something has to change, though, because it is obviously coming, and it is getting closer. I'm not sure how long I have, but I fear that before too long, it may not matter what precautions I take… it will get in.

10 Adulting

I had just moved out of my childhood home and into my very first rental house. The excitement I felt to begin this new chapter in my life had no words.

As a child, you daydream what life will be like when you get to begin your own. I dreamt of white picket fences, a cute little puppy, or falling in love and starting a family. The possibilities were endless.

Obviously, as an adult, you realize life is much different from your daydreams and you have to save longer for the white picket fence... but I found myself a true gem.

It was tucked into an older cul-de-sac in an area of town where I could walk to mostly anything, including school. It was perfect. It even had a second bedroom (although small) for an office or craft room.

During the first week of unpacking and arranging the house, one of my best friends Mandy came over to see the new place.

I had not really had time to splurge on a nice dining table yet, so we sat on the sofa and ordered in some Chinese.

Awhile after eating and giggling about college life, Mandy went into my master bedroom to check out the layout. I noticed right away the door to the master bath was shut. This was odd since I was the only one that lived there, and I never shut it.

When I attempted to open the bathroom door to show her inside, it was locked. Again, really peculiar.

I looked at Mandy. I was obviously confused but Mandy merely shrugged her shoulders. "It's ok, show me later when you find a key," she said.

I shook my head in disbelief and we started to trot out of the room.

Then a noise stopped us just under the door frame. It was the sound of the shower curtain opening.

Mandy turned to me and whispered, "No one else is here, right?" But of course she already knew I was the only one who lived there.

I slowly shook my head, shivering and trying not to be terrified.

We glanced over our shoulders at the still closed door and went back out into the living room and called the police.

Mandy and I waited outside for the police to arrive. I was extremely stressed, nipping at my nails and pacing. Could there be someone in my bathroom?

We had been eating and talking for nearly two hours before going into my bedroom. Could a person hide that long? And what did they want?

The police arrived and we followed, pointing the way to the bathroom. A policewoman who was tall and slender with "take charge" written all over her face grabbed the door handle to the bathroom and it opened right away.

Mandy gasped. I stood there eternally perplexed. Were we going crazy?

We watched as their flashlights encircled the entirety of the bathroom. There was nothing in there.

The policewoman put her flashlight down by her side, noting no visible threat. "Is this a joke?"

We both vigorously shook our heads. "No ma'am. Something was in there."

She scoffed and walked with her partner outside. Obviously, she didn't believe us at all. After an outside perimeter check revealed no obvious signs of an attempted break-in they were gone, and we were left shrouded in our own disbelief.

Mandy offered for me to stay at her house for the night just so I could get the incident off my mind and start fresh tomorrow. It was not hard for me to agree to that!

After one last sweep of my house, I grabbed what I needed for class, turned off all the lights and locked up.

The next morning, I had gone straight to class before going home. Finally, around lunchtime I had enough time to run home, drop off some textbooks and grab a couple others before my next class.

I hung my keys by the front door and made my way to my bedroom. I sat my textbooks from my earlier classes on my dresser and grabbed the ones I needed for my afternoon classes.

I suddenly felt a chill. I shivered. Then I felt like I was being watched. I tried to shrug it off as anxiety from what had happened from the night before until my gaze fell to my bed. My bed was made as I had left it, only there was an imprint on it of an entire person. It was as if someone had laid on it and taken a nap. That had definitely not been me!

I grabbed my books and ran out of there as fast as I could, almost forgetting to grab my keys off of the hook by the front door.

I called Mandy and told her all about it. I was seriously freaked out. Mandy suggested she stay the night with me so I didn't have to be alone and maybe it would help me adjust to my new place better.

Mandy came over that evening after school. She brought popcorn and a couple movies and a bottle of wine.

Finally, after two movies we were both getting exhausted. I turned off the t.v. and the lights and we went to bed. Mandy was sleeping in my bed with me because I had a queen.

We lay down and we are talking a little bit about school and guys. Most of the events that had happened in the house were far from my mind by. I was completely exhausted but at ease.

We both drifted off to sleep. Suddenly, I was awakened in the middle of the night and gazed at my bedside clock. Two-thirteen a.m. I could not figure out why I woke up, so I searched the darkness for answers.

Seeing and hearing nothing, I rolled over on my side to face Mandy. Even though the room was dark, I could see it. Somehow, its form was darker than the room.

It was the shape of a person but with no legs, and it hovered almost all the way to the height of the ceiling. I blinked my eyes to focus better. Still there. It sounded like it was hissing, or growling. I couldn't discern which.

Too scared to call out for her, I tried to nudge Mandy awake with my foot under the covers. Nothing. She slept on.

My heart was pounding. I was terrified the thing was going to attack her. So, I nudged her again harder while keeping my eyes on the thing.

Finally, she stirred and blinked her eyes at me. She started to sit up, "Why did you kick me?"

My eyes must have been about ready to pop out of my head in terror. I was trying my best to tell her with my eyes, while in a pitch-black room, to shut up and run. But she just kept looking at me for answers.

I looked over again at the darkness that was still hovering right next to her. Without a second to answer I just yelled, "Run!"

The covers were tossed aside and we were both pounding footfalls out of my bedroom and into my living room.

Breathless, she asked me, "What are we running from?"

I was flipping on every light in the house at this point while she was trailing behind me.

"The thing by the bed. It was right next to you!"

Her eyes grew wide in horror. "Wha—What thing?"

"It was as tall as the ceiling."

Whatever it was did not follow us into the living room. We stayed there the remainder of the night with every light in the house on.

The next morning, I moved back in with my parents and broke my lease.

I could not handle another night in that house.

11 Necrosis

Funeral homes did not scare me. I was around them since I can remember. My dad worked at one, as did his dad, and so on. I guess you could say "It runs in the family."

It was around ten o'clock in the evening and I was getting ready to call it a night, when the county coroner brought in a suicide victim.

I was drinking a cup of warm coffee and flipping through the file I just received on our newest intake. I had to have been looking at the file for well over a half-hour when the lights in my office began to flicker.

I thought it was strange, but technically the building was not exactly youthful, so I just brushed it off.

I continued flipping through the file and reading the death certificate. I kept thinking about how tragic it was. She was only twenty and she wanted it all to be over. What could have been so horrible that you felt you had to end it all before life even began?

I slurped down the last few drops of my coffee and rose from my chair. As I did so, the hairs on the back of my neck stood at attention and I got the chills. I felt like someone was watching me.

I told myself I was being silly. I've had tons of cases like this before and easily ignored the "willies." I walked out of my office and into the embalming room.

As I neared the table to begin the embalming process, I could not shake the feeling I was being observed. I rubbed at my eyes and cracked my knuckles. I had this. I totally had this.

Suddenly, I was overwhelmed with emotion. My eyes began to tear up and I braced a hand on the table so I could collect myself and not begin to cry. What was happening to me tonight?

Just as I took my hand off of the table and cleared my throat, a scalpel fell off of one of the trays and loudly onto the floor. I stood there frozen, staring at it for a moment, still overwhelmed with the urge to cry.

Then the smell began. The utter smell of necrosis. It was a stench that burnt my nostrils to their core. It was everything I could do to hold back the gag seeping up my throat.

I turned every which way, hopeful to see something that was causing the stench, but there was nothing. I was still alone.

I finally had it. After a few minutes, the smell only seemed to grow stronger. I called someone else in so I could go home. I was completely rattled, and I needed some sleep.

The next morning, I went back into work and asked my friend who relieved me if anything unusual had happened to him. He peered at me skeptically and said, "No."

So eventually I chalked it up to my imagination. I never had an experience like it again. Maybe I was just too tired. But anytime I smell necrosis my mind immediately plays back that night with the suicide victim.

12 Mirror mirror

Have you ever looked into a mirror at night and wondered if it is really you that is staring back at you? Do the shadows hide a truth that is too horrible to accept, one that will change everything from that moment on? It is said that spirits can use mirrors for travel or to communicate with this world. This is something I didn't know when a friend and I decided we wanted to try performing a seance together to see if we could communicate with something not of this world. We thought that we were safe. We thought it was no big deal. We were wrong.

My friend Alexis was spending the night with me that night. Her parents were out of town, and they didn't want her to be in the house by herself. Really, they didn't trust her not to throw some sort of party while they were gone was the truth of the matter. They had a right to be warry since that is exactly what would have happened, but I was thrilled to have one of my best friends staying with me for a week. We had all sorts of plans from movies, makeovers, and best of all, a night that we planned on performing a seance. We checked out a few websites that gave instructions on how to do one, and we thought it sounded creepy and cool. Because it was going to be the highlight of the stay, we thought we would wait until the last night, but neither one of us wanted to wait, so we decided it would be the perfect way to kick things off with a bang.

It was nearly midnight, and we had everything set up. We had found a script online of words to say to contact spirits and had printed off two copies so we could speak the words together. We had also brought candles and a few crystals that my mom had around the house. She claimed they were for protection. I just thought they looked cool. We set up in front of my closet, which had mirrored doors. We had read that spirits could use mirrors to travel and communicate, so we figured it couldn't hurt our chances.

We took turns lighting the candles we had in front of us. The wicks caught quickly, and we were bathed in the soft glowing light. At this point, Alexis went and turned off the lamp in the room, which was the only other source of illumination other than the candles at the time. We then sat down and started to recite the chant that we had selected. After the first time, we sat there silent, listening for any sound that could indicate that something might be there with us. My entire body was tingling with fear and anticipation. This didn't seem like such a good idea anymore, and I was hoping nothing would happen.

Alexis looked around the room before meeting my eyes. I could see the flame of the candle reflecting in them. "Let's try again and see what happens."

As much as I didn't want to, nothing happening the first time bolstered my confidence that this wasn't going to lead to anything more than me getting myself worked up about nothing. So once again, we started our chant, calling forth any spirit to come forth and speak with us, to let their presence be known.

I sat there waiting for something to happen, but I no longer believed what we were doing was real. What were we thinking anyway? We were just a couple of teenagers talking to some candles and rocks. The candles' flames didn't move, no strange temperature changes happened, no tapping or knocking noises occurred, just silence. I let go of a breath that I didn't know I was holding and felt relief rush over me.

I looked over into the mirror at myself; my reflection stared back at me just like it always did. I glanced over at the space in the mirror where Alexis' reflection was, and her reflection looked much the same as mine did, looking as if her head was turned toward the mirror. Something about it seemed wrong, though, but why? The realization hit me like I had been slapped. It was wrong because Alexis wasn't looking towards the mirror. She was facing me; only her reflection was turned towards her.

I began to shiver uncontrollably as fear pounded through every part of my body. This wasn't real; my mind was playing tricks on me. The face in the mirror turned towards me and its mouth curved into a smile that split her face from ear to ear.

The mouth began to move, but I didn't hear anything inside my head but two words. "Hello, Josie."

The candles flickered violently, and then they were snuffed out, casting the room in complete darkness. I started to hear scurrying noises all around me. In the pitch black, I couldn't tell where they were coming from or what was there with us. Every nerve in my body felt like it was humming as adrenaline surged through my blood. I felt a slight breeze as something got close to me and shuffled by.

I reach out in front of me, trying to feel for the familiar shapes in my room as I crawl blindly forward. It seems like I crawl farther than my room is long, but I finally feel something solid in front of me. It feels like it could be the sheets on my bed as I move my hands across the surface. At first, I think it is my sheets, but it is greasy and cold. I pull my hand back, but even after letting go, the slick substance clings to my fingers.

A slight breeze tickles the fine hairs around my ear, and I hear a sound like a wet sucking noise coming from behind me. Whatever is here in my room is right there, inches from the back of my head. The sound comes closer, and I realize what I am hearing, it is its breath. The mouth of whatever this thing may be is right next to my ear. The smell of rotten eggs assaults my nose, and I gag from the smell. My breath shudders as I inhale, and I bite my lip, trying to keep from crying out.

The breathing draws back from my ear, and the room becomes silent. I still haven't heard any noise from Alexis or know how far away from her I am right now. I turn my head from side to side, straining to hear the slightest noise but can't make anything out in the void.

The pain alone steals the breath from my lungs, rendering me unable to scream or even make a sound. I have to get out of here, but I don't know which way I have to go. The dark has robbed me of any sense of where I am in my room. Lost, I begin to crawl in a random direction, desperate to get away. I swing my hand back and forth in an arc, trying to find the wall, my bed, anything.

Finally, my hand comes into contact with something solid. I run it across its surface and realize I have found one of the walls of my bedroom. Using it as a guide, I follow it moving slowly, brushing my fingers against it to remain on course while my other hand prods forward into the dark. I'm hoping to find the door, but instead, I bump my hand against another wall and find myself in one of the corners of my bedroom.

I wedge myself into the corner and face the emptiness in front of me. Just having the wall behind me made me feel safer. At least now, I didn't think something could get me from behind.

Although I can't see it, I hear movement coming towards me, this time though, it doesn't sound like it is on the floor but rather on the wall or maybe the ceiling above me. It is slow and methodical; whatever this thing is, it knows I'm cornered, and it is taking its time, enjoying itself.

I didn't realize at the time I'd made a mistake. I hadn't found a safe place but rather cut off my means of escape. Now I was trapped, and it was coming closer. The sound of the movement stopped. It seemed as if it could have been right on top of me when the room fell silent. I focused everything I had, trying to hear where it was.

From somewhere above me, a cold, wet drip hits my forehead and slides down the side of my face. I reach a hand up and touch the liquid. It is greasy. A cold dread spreads through me as I realize it is right above me. In an act of desperation, I bolt from the corner of my room toward where I believe the door is. I stumble and fall over obstacles as I rush in blind panic towards what I hope is safety. The wet sucking noise seems to be right over my shoulder.

I crash into the wall, and I flail my arms across it, looking for the door and my escape. I move to the right, praying I am going in the right direction. Thankfully my hand bumps into the doorframe, and I scramble to find the knob. Finally, my hand finds what I'm looking for, and I twist it hard and throw myself out into the hall, landing hard on my elbow and hip.

I look back where I had just come from, the light from the hallway barely illuminates my room, but there is enough light to see a dark shadow floating near the ceiling through my door. In a blink, it flashes away and is out of sight.

I stand and walk back to the door, Alexis is still in there, and I don't want to leave her. I quickly reach my hand around the corner and flip the switch on the wall bathing the room in light. I see her lying on the floor near where she had been when the lights went out. I rush over to her and roll her over onto her back. I see she has several red welts all over her arms, legs, and across her face. She moans weakly and opens her eyes to me.

"Alexis, are you okay?"

All I get from her is a slight nod, and then she cringes as if even that caused her a great deal of pain. Whatever was in the room had hurt her pretty badly. I lifted her up slowly onto the bed and got her situated so she would be as comfortable as possible. I didn't sleep at all for the rest of the night. I kept the light on, trying to keep the shadow at bay.

The next morning Alexis woke up sore, but the welts seemed to be fading. We found a ritual to perform that was supposed to banish evil spirits online and performed it, hoping that would get rid of what had attacked us the night before.

I am pleased to report that I haven't come into contact with my tormentor from that night again. Whether it was the ritual we performed, or it was just done with us, we haven't seen it since. We also don't try and contact spirits or anything else not of this world. After the experience that night, we realized how ill-prepared we were when we did that and left ourselves open to being harmed. What started out as something we intended to be fun ended up being my worst nightmare, one we are not willing to repeat.

13 Shadow at the fair

Every year my city has a county fair. We have all been to one of these things at least once in our lives. We also know that if you have been one year, you can pretty much assume it will be exactly the same the next. As a teen, I did not really enjoy going because none of the things I could do there held much interest for me. Everything was for adults or little kids, so I usually found myself bored out of my mind. That was until I turned 17 and my boyfriend and I decided to go together. It turned into a night I will never forget.

I was so excited to go to the fair for the first time in years. My boyfriend Scott was taking me out on a date there. We were still in the honeymoon phase of our relationship, and I wanted to be around him as much as I could. It was going to be the first time I had ever been able to go to the annual event with someone other than my parents, and I was looking forward to spending some alone time with Scott.

We planned on eating dinner at the fair, so he picked me up around 5:00 pm. We parked the car and walked hand in hand to go buy our tickets. Once inside, we walked over to the food court and decided on something to eat. It is funny, though, how a corn dog can feel like a romantic dinner when shared with the right person. As nice as it was to be close to Scott, my stomach suddenly started to hurt, and I felt like I was going to throw up. I had felt perfectly fine just minutes before, and I had not been feeling sick earlier in the day, so I could not really explain why I all of a sudden felt so poorly. It was like I got a case of the chills out of nowhere.

I figured that the greasy food had upset my stomach and just brushed it off. Not wanting to tempt the rides too quickly, we decided to walk around and check out the local vendor booths. When we were at the animal shelter's booth petting the dogs that they had available for adoption, I had this overwhelming feeling like someone was watching me. I stood up and turned around in a circle, trying to find the culprit. I thought I could see someone facing in my direction, but it was hard to tell because where they were standing, they seemed to be cloaked in shadows, so I could not tell for sure. The person seemed to be wearing an odd hat, like a top hat, which is why he stood out so much to me. When I looked in their direction, the feeling of being looked at seemed to intensify.

I just told Scott I wanted to go somewhere else, and he gave me a look like he didn't understand because he knows how much I like animals but being the guy he is, he didn't object. As we were walking away, I kept looking over my shoulder, trying to see if we were being followed. I thought I saw the person a couple of times, but in the throngs of people around us, I was not sure. By this time, Scott had noticed my odd behavior and asked what I was looking at. I knew how it would sound, but I told him that I thought someone was following us. In typical Scott fashion, he did what most people would do, he turned around and had a look for himself. He asked me what the person looked like, but all I could tell him was about the hat and that I only saw him in the shadows. Obviously, this was not much help, so he told me he would keep an eye out.

We decided that I needed something fun to take my mind off things, so the carnival seemed to be the best thing to do that. A couple of rides would put me in a better mood, I thought. In the back of my mind, I just could not shake the feeling that the person was still out there. I kept scanning back and forth looking for them, but whether it was just paranoia, or he was really there, every shadow seemed to take the shape of the watcher.

I was getting really creeped out at this point, but I still wanted to have a good time, so I agreed to go on the Ferris wheel. The line was not exceptionally long, so it only took a couple of minutes before we were being loaded onto one of the cars. I remember going up into the air and feeling a sense of relief pass over me; he could not get me here. The moment was short-lived, though, because when we came around the backside of the ride, I could see the man in the top hat standing in line for the ride we were on. I shook Scott by the shoulder and pointed him out. I could feel him stiffen next to me as he seemed to realize I was not just making it up. As we came around to the front, I tried to see any recognizable features, but even in the bright sunlight, he just seemed to be made completely out of shadows. The other thing I noticed, no one else seemed to be paying it any attention. If Scott had not seen it too, I might have thought I was seeing things. The scary thing about it, though, was when the ride spun around again, the shadow was briefly blocked by one of the carts, then when the area came back into view, it was gone, like it had never been there.

Both of us were a bit shook up by this occurrence, but it was still early, and I was not going to let some weirdo ruin our date. The problem with that idea was we both seemed to see him everywhere we went, riding a horse on the carousel, standing at a game to win a stuffed animal, or just peeking out at us from a dark corner. This went on throughout the evening and into the night. I got more and more scared while Scott just seemed to get angry. He would think he saw something out of the corner of his eye and go charging after it only to come up empty-handed every time.

So, we decided something that in hindsight was a stupid thing, we decided to go into the funhouse. Scott figured he could confront the guy following us around and get him to quit, and what better place to do it than an enclosed area where the guy could not just disappear.

As we are standing in line to get admitted, I start to second guess this plan of ours. Why weren't we just leaving the fair? I mean, why put us in a potentially dangerous situation? If this guy was willing to stalk us all over the fair, he obviously was not right in the head, so why give him a chance to get close to us? I mentioned this to Scott, but at this point, he was so frustrated that he had convinced himself he had to do this and would not listen to reason.

I was not going to leave him to go in by himself, plus I did not feel safe walking out alone, so I decided to go inside with him. Let me tell you, the place was disorienting enough as is, but add on top of it, you're scared out of your wits because you think some guy is going to jump out and grab you at any moment the place seemed to take on another level of messed up.

When we got to the room with the funhouse mirrors, things went from bad to worse. Scott and I were looking at each other's reflections in the various mirrors when behind me, I noticed the silhouette of the man in the top hat. I spun around, ready to face my tormentor, but no one was there, just the wall behind me. I turned back to the mirror, expecting to see nothing more than my reflection but there again was the man, but this time he was moving towards me with his arms outstretched like he intended to grab me. Scott seemed to sense my fear and investigated the mirror I was standing in front of. He saw the shadow figure coming towards me and spun to face it down, but like me, all he saw was the empty room.

At this point, I was so scared all I could do was stare at the reflection as it came closer and closer to me. Finally, I was within arm's reach, and I watched as it closed its fingers around my shoulders. Pain shot through me, it was like I was being burned, but instead of it being hot, it was freezing cold. I could see my breath, and my teeth were chattering, granted I do not know if I was shivering from the cold or just fear. It moved it hands up towards my throat; the freezing cold hands seemed to wrap around my throat, and I started to have trouble breathing. I could not move. All I could do was stand there and let it happen.

From the side, it felt like something was trying to pull my shoulder out of its socket. I looked over in that direction, and Scott had grabbed my arm and was pulling me out of the room as quickly as he could. I stumbled along behind him, not fully back to normal. From behind me, I heard some sort of inhuman shriek of anger. I did not look back for fear of what was back there. Later Scott told me he had not heard anything, so I am not sure if this was just in my head. Fortunately, this was one of the last rooms, and we burst through the door back into the outside air.

Neither one of us had any interest in staying at the fair for another second. We got quite a few angry looks as we bulled our way through the crowds and out into the parking lot as fast as we could. Get away, just get away was the only thing on either of our minds. We hit the car at a dead run and, after fumbling with his keys for a few seconds, unlocked our doors. We jumped in and took off out of there as fast as we could, desperate to put distance between us and whatever was back at the fair.

To this day, I still have not ever gone back to the county fair. I just felt lucky that whatever Scott and I encountered that day did not or could not follow us home. Every once in a while, when I get that feeling that I'm being watched, I flashback to that time at the fair, and I wonder, is it that same hatted man, has he found me, and will I be so lucky this time?

14 In the Vents

The experts that supposedly know why people become ghosts say it happens for a variety of reasons, violent deaths, unfinished business, maybe even that they do not know that they are dead yet. Despite the reason for the death, some of them are more tragic than others. Fewer might be considered more so than the reason my apartment building had been haunted for more than two decades. I guess I'll start at the end first and let you know why the building was haunted, then I'll tell you about some of the events that a number of tenants experienced while living there.

I watched as they wheeled the gurney out of the front of my building. I did not see the reason for it considering Amber had been dead for over twenty years. When a child dies, especially one as young as her, it is a monumental tragedy. How did we find out this little girl's body had been in the ventilation system that long? The answer is simple yet hard to believe; she had been haunting our building for the eight years I had lived here, and it had been going on for longer than that. I figured it would be a good idea to tell the stories of all the people that had some contact with Amber, or at least what they think is contact.

Amber was reported to have lived in the building with her parents back in the late eighties. One day she was reported missing by her mother, and the police did an investigation but were unable to find out what had happened to her or even the whereabouts of her body. After several weeks, the case was abandoned, and she became another runway child that probably would never be found.

Another set of people staying here had several instances where they described the sound like someone grabbing hold of the vents in the hallways and shaking them with a great deal of force, enough so they would have expected the drywall to be cracked. When they would go and inspect the location, though, nothing would be out of place.

Although I could never figure out when the haunting actually started, the earliest experience I could find happened about one year from the time of her disappearance. The people used to live in the apartment right next to where Amber and her family lived. They said they heard scratching coming from inside the walls. They told me it was like someone was taking their fingernails and slowly dragging it across the entire length of the wall at a time. When I asked them if they possibly could have heard mice or rats moving in the walls since, after all, this was a big city, and the building was older; they told me they had thought about that, they had even had the landlord hire an exterminator to come and look, but no droppings or anything else was found to back up that possibility. They said the noise happened for nearly a decade before it finally stopped.

Later, one of the more disturbing stories actually came from inside the apartment itself, where Amber used to live. One group of tenants was reportedly scared so badly, they ran off and broke their lease to get away from it. I was told that they would see dirty black fingers reaching out of the rooms' heating vents like someone was stuck there and trying to get into the rooms. They would sit there and listen as something would start tapping at the metal, sometimes for a minute sometimes for over an hour. This went on until they would go and inspect the vents. When they would look inside, most of the time, there would not be anything there. However, on a few occasions, there are stories that a young girl's face would be looking back at them with pale white skin. When they saw her the second time, they made a choice to pack up and leave in the middle of the night.

I found several stories that are similar throughout the building, but what got me interested in other people's experiences was not just watching them finally find the girl in the vents, but my own experiences. The first time I had something happen to me was about a month after I had moved in. On occasion, I would hear the sound of a young child giggling coming from inside of the vents. At first, I did not think anything of it because I just assumed it was coming from the adjacent unit, thinking that the people must have a little girl. One day I had run into the people next to me, and I noticed they did not have any kids with them. I asked them where their daughter was. They gave me a funny look and told me that they did not have any children. I was perplexed because I know what I had heard and asked them if someone had visited with them that did. At this point, I was starting to irritate them with all my questions, and they abruptly told me there had not been any kids in their place and stormed off.

About a year later, I came back from work, ready to relax after a hard day at work. The incident with the giggles coming from the vent had long since been forgotten. I walked into my room, and I noticed that the heating vent on the floor had been pushed up and was laying on the floor on its side. The first thing I was worried about was that some sort of rodent had come through into my place, and now I would have to find where it had gone, so it didn't cause any damage. As I left my room to start my search, it only took me walking into the next room, which happened to be my living room, to notice that the two vents in here had also been pushed out and left haphazardly on the floor. This got me thinking that someone may have come in here doing some sort of inspection. I walked from room to room, and I found the same thing, every vent had been removed and left on the ground. Now in my rental agreement, the landlord had the right to come in and inspect with no notice if it was a utility issue, so after replacing all the vent covers, I called the office manager. What he told me, though, did not make any sense; he said that no one had gone into my place that day. I asked him how my vents ended up on the ground, but he did not seem to know or have any explanation for it.

I started to think that there might be rats in the place like one of the previous people had because I constantly heard a scraping noise coming from the ducts behind the walls. It sounded like something was pulling itself through the vent system. The problem with it being rats or maybe some other kind of small animal was the metal would bend and flex when it moved, which meant that either it was the biggest rat in history or something big was in there, too big to have gotten in there on its own.

On a few occasions, I even thought that I spotted eyes peering out at me, staring when I was not paying attention. I would see them out of the corner of my eyes, but when I would turn directly toward them, nothing would be there. The place was unsettling. No matter where you went in the building, I never could get comfortable, I could never relax.

What finally got me to call someone to take a closer look in the system and eventually to the discovery of Amber's remains happened only recently. I was in my kitchen making dinner when I heard someone scream. It was the scream of a young girl, and it was coming from the vent. I yelled down into it, asking if she was okay, but all I got in return was cries again and again as if she were in excruciating pain. I told her I was going to call the police and ran to the phone. The dispatcher seemed not to believe me at first, but they must have heard the panic in my voice and thought twice about asking me if this was some sort of prank.

The firetrucks and ambulance showed up pretty quickly and began getting to work. By this time, the screaming had ceased, and I was afraid that they were too late to do anything to help whoever was down there. After not being able to get a response from someone in the vent, they decided to feed a camera down to see if they could see anything. After only a few minutes, I heard one of the rescuers say something; the only thing I could make out from where I was at was the word 'bones'. I did not know it at the time, but they had discovered Amber's body in the ventilation system and the source of all the paranormal happenings in the building.

What happened next was a rush of activity. Men were cutting a hole in the wall somewhere downstairs so they could extract the remains. We were all instructed to wait outside while they removed the remains, which is how I got outside when the paramedics removed Amber from our building on the gurney.

Once her bones had been removed, the building seemed to take on a lighter feeling over the next couple of days. I believe that Amber's spirit was stuck in that building because someone had dumped her body, and she was a restless spirit. It was a few weeks before we actually found out who the person was that had been found in the ducts, but due to decomposition, the police really didn't have much evidence to figure out what had happened to her. I have my own theories based upon hearing the screaming coming from the vent that night, but paranormal experiences are not admissible in court. To this day, I have not heard or seen any of the strange things that seemed to be part of living in that building, which I take as Amber has moved on. I am happy that she is now in a better place.

15 The creeper

Most shadow people, to my knowledge, are quick to run if you look directly at them. They will linger in dark corners or even closets, watching intently from afar. My shadow person was quite relentless for about a year, and his torment began when I was six years old.

In the beginning, it started as something out of the corner of my eye, easily brushed off as a figment of my imagination. Then it evolved into a curious stare from around a corner. Later it progressed to wavering in my open doorway, creeping slowly towards me and faltering at the end of my bed, glaring. And finally, the paralysis began.

After its progression, when it had mustered the apparent courage to glide into my room, the air became heavy and tense. I'd watch him slowly glide in and cower at the end of my bed, and no matter how terrified I was, I could not beg my eyes to shut. Once the paralysis let up enough for me to move, I'd claw at my bedding, trembling in fear and pull it tightly over my head.

Quite a few minutes would pass, then I would feel the air in the room get lighter, and the tension begin to ease. I'd slowly, then lower the covers down to my chin to find the figure dissipated. My eyes would dart about the room in a thorough inspection of the space, but he'd be long gone.

As most common shadow people have been reported, mine was different than most. He did not wear a hat, nor was he cloaked in a hood. Instead, he was a black outline of a man that was fully black with fuzzy edges.

During this year of the most frequent shadow visits, I began to have a reoccurring dream of a hooded man. I would find myself in a desolate neighborhood on the blackest of nights, the smell of burning wood and plastic hovering in the air in every direction. I'd look down at my feet and notice I was perched on a sidewalk. Once taking in my surroundings, I'd see the entire neighborhood was on fire. Flames licking out of windows like devilish tongues, but none of this would be audible. I expected sirens, or screams, or crackling embers, but it was like someone had hit the mute button.

After gaining some courage, I'd walk from the sidewalk into the street towards the scorching buildings. I'd reach the lawn of one of the engulfed homes and see my brother standing idly in the yard with a frozen stare on his face. He'd stare at the flames as if mesmerized by their creation.

Calling his name was useless, he could never hear me, so I'd venture closer little by little until my hand was on his shoulder, trying to shake him out of his trance. Then, it was as if breaking his daze unmuted the world. The sound of aching wood, bending metal, and crackling fire would engulf my eardrums to such a high velocity that I would pull my hand back from his shoulder to shield my ears from the noise.

This heavy feeling of terror and doom would seep into my spine like a snake traveling up towards my neck. This sensation was accompanied by a heavy pressure as if someone were standing right against my back. I just knew that something was lurking behind us.

With my hands still sheltering my ears, I'd turn around to see a cloaked shadow figure inches from me with glowing amber eyes. His eyes would glow brighter and brighter crimson, as if they were controlled by dimmer light switches, which were slowly being turned on high, followed by a mind-splitting growl before I would wake trembling in sweat-soaked sheets.

After that year, the shadow man just disappeared. I felt like I had my life back. Obviously, with the suddenness of his departure and with no reasoning behind it, I was still on eggshells. But after a while, I eased and quit looking over my shoulder. Even the house felt less heavy. It was as if someone had opened a window and ventilated the air; it was cleaner.

A few months ago, I turned twenty. I had just begun my sophomore year at college, and after a few years of only casual relationships, I'd finally settled into a committed relationship with my current boyfriend, Troy.

Troy is a non-believer. He thinks ghosts are silly and made up, and because of this, I had not told him about my shadow experiences from my past. Honestly, I didn't think there was a need to. That was, until a few months ago, when my life turned upside down again.

It was a Friday night; moments before, we'd arrived home from a friends' party, and we had just fallen asleep in his bed. I was awoken by Troy whimpering in his sleep and thrashing around. Because he only had a twin-size bed, I felt myself falling off of his bed on numerous occasions. Once I'd positioned myself in a sturdy place on his bed to avoid his trouncing, I attempted to shake him awake.

My heart was pounding in my ears, and anxiety was riding up in my chest to my throat. Since my experiences as a child, I'm often terrified of the dark, and his horrible nightmare was freaking me out. Before he could wake, I felt it. It was like a fog of heaviness had descended upon the room and had crept closer to the bed.

My hands retreated from his body, and all attempts to stir him were abandoned. I had a sudden urge to steer my attention to his closet as if something was pleading with me to be seen.

At first, through the veil of darkness of his room, it appeared like any other normal closet. His clothes were hung on the upper rack, and others were folded inside the cubbies below. Then for a split second, I saw something twitch. I blinked and squinted, my eyes refusing to believe there was something inside.

That's when I saw them. From behind his neat line of hung shirts, there were two dull, hazy purple eyes staring back at me. The more I stared, the more he came into focus. His hazy blackened body blended so eerily well with the dimness of the room, but yet, I could loosely make out most of him. He seemed to be wearing a hat, almost a complete form of a man, and those sinister muddled purple eyes were glowering at me through the darkness.

By this time, Troy had already long ended his nightmare thrashing and was again sleeping peacefully beside me. I sat there upright on the bed, my eyes trained on the closet, and its sinister contents for what I imagined was at least ten minutes. I held back my urge to call out to Troy in my throat and listened intently for movement from the closet.

Suddenly, in a panic at the first sign of movement, I jerked my gaze towards the bedroom door as it slowly seemed to open by itself. My hands clawed the sheets, and my heart raced in terrified silence. Just as it had opened about a foot, Buddy, Troy's Terrier, padded in slowly and headed for his normal spot at the foot of the bed. I let out a loud sigh with the breath I'd been holding and turned back towards the closet and the evil it had held inside, but the hatted shadow had disappeared.

After that night, whenever I spent the night at Troy's, I'd see him. Whether it was out of the corner of my eye, peering around a corner or again in the room by the doorway or in the closet, he'd be there… watching me.

A few months came and went, and my anxiety was out of control. I wanted to tell Troy what I'd been seeing, but I just didn't think he would understand, let alone believe me. We were early in our relationship, and I didn't want to ruin it. I really liked him.

I decided to go on the internet and search for what I'd been seeing to gain some answers. I found so many different stories of hatted shadows, but none with purple eyes. My heart sank. I started to feel so alone and helpless. I knew he wasn't harming me physically, but the shadow was harming me mentally.

Finally, after scouring the internet to no avail, I went outside on Troy's back patio to lay out and enjoy a glass of lemonade. I needed to get my mind off of the shadow. It seemed to be the only thing I could focus on these days.

I listened to the bird's chirp and the sounds of distant traffic and let my eyes close. Before long, I heard a low clattering from the kitchen, opened my eyes, and turned and peered at the sliding glass doors to see if the noise was coming from Troy. It was. His blurred figure was crouched down half bent inside the fridge.

As I was about to turn back around, I saw the oddest thing. I had to squint my eyes due to the sunlight to focus it properly. These black particles seemed to bounce off one another but, at the same time, come together to form the dark shadow man. I watched in horror as right behind the glass, inside the apartment, it formed.

By this time, I just thought I was nuts, and I probably needed to go to the doctor to get on some sort of medication or something. This couldn't be normal to be seeing things like this all the time. Either I was starting to go crazy, or something evil was living in my boyfriend's apartment and was targeting only me.

Intently, refusing to turn my attention around, I watched. Troy popped his bottle cap off of his beer and headed for the glass door to join me outside. The shadow just sat there watching me. Once Troy approached the door and extended an arm out to open it, the shadow collapsed in on itself and dissipated. The strangest thing is the whole time Troy was walking towards the door; he didn't seem to see anything. He came outside all casual and chipper and sat beside me. The whole time I'm still in shock and completely dumbfounded as to how he did not just see that creepy thing inches from him before he opened that door!

That day was the last day I spent at my boyfriend's apartment. Due to all of the mixed emotions of staying over there, I was barely sleeping, hardly eating, and feeling as if I were headed for some sort of mental breakdown. I ended our relationship and decided to move forward with my life.

I don't remember exactly how long it had been since we had broken up, a month or so maybe, but I had received a text late one evening from a mutual friend of Troy, and I. Troy had been struck by another vehicle on his way home from class and was killed. Frankly, I was devastated and a little creeped out.

It took quite a while to heal from that and put it past me, but I did. A few years passed, and I graduated and began my career as a vet tech. I loved my job even though the hours were sometimes insane, and emergencies were quite often. But I always volunteered to come in and help out no matter what hour of the night.

I wish I could say through all of what had happened so far, the shadows were gone, and my life was refreshed, and all of the craziness was behind me. But it wasn't. The next time I saw a shadow, it actually all started to make sense.

It was on my day off, and winter was just coming to an end. I'd gone to my grandma's house to spend some time with her as she was starting to get ill quite often, and we weren't sure how much time she had left.

She'd insisted on teaching me how to crochet. Practically forced the needle and yarn in my hand. I sat on the floor below her favorite recliner while she perched in her recliner and guided me step by step.

We were interrupted by three knocks at the front door. I scooted my butt backward to allow her the space to get up and answer the door.

"Well, that's odd," she hobbled back towards her chair.

"What is?"

She shrugged as she seated herself and placed the yarn back on her lap, "No one was there."

I busied myself with the double stitch she'd taught me, "Apparently, whatever it was wasn't that important."

She giggled as she ran her hook back through her yarn.

I started to struggle with the double stitch, and looked up at her, opened my mouth to ask for help, but nothing came out by shock.

Behind her chair was the hatted shadow from my boyfriend's house. The one I hadn't seen in years. The one who had me living in silent torment for nearly a year.

"What is it, honey?" My grandma leaned forward, eyeing me, her forehead creased with concern.

I quickly tried to act as naturally as possible as not to frighten my grandma. "It's nothing. I'm just a little over-tired."

She nodded and eased back in her chair, returning to her task. She peered over her thick glasses at her yarn and hummed while she stitched. I, on the other hand, eyed the shadow out of the corner of my eye as I pretended it wasn't really there, all the while silently jealous of her lack of concern.

That particular visit with my grandma started everything all over again. My anxiety returned double fold. I was scared to even leave the house for fear I would see something out of the corner of my eye at work and be unable to hide my fear.

After calling in sick for three days, I received a phone call from my mother at seven in the morning. Her voice was urgent, slightly breaking, and raspy. In my entire life, I've never heard my mom sound like she did at that moment, and it made my blood run as cold as ice.

While I listened to her explain that my grandmother had passed away earlier that morning, I just knew.

Something connects the shadow to tragedies. And for some reason, I'm the only one that can see them. I'm still in search of answers as to why this is happening to me, and I have no clue how this connects back to when I was six and who died then. As much as I recall, there were no close family or friend deaths at that time in my life. It just seems that when something bad is coming, they appear. And not only do I see them, they see me too.

16 Behind you

Since I am what they call, "a spiritual empath," I can sense bad energy from a person, place, or object. Mostly I am sensitive to auras, but on occasion, I can also pick up on spirits, usually the bad ones.

My sister and her husband had just bought a new house and were going on a week-long vacation to Italy. They asked if I'd house sit since they had not had a chance to have their alarm system set up yet.

The first night was a breeze. I enjoyed having all the space to myself as I had roommates at my apartment; I delighted in the quiet of the place.

On the second night, however, things began to get strange. No matter where I walked through the house, I felt a coldness at my back, as if something was following me. But only at my backside; the rest of the room was cozy and warm. Then my senses started to kick in, and I began to feel as if there was a very tall entity following me, trying to intimidate me.

By the next morning, I tried to shrug it off as over-reading the auras in her house, as nothing had happened after I went to bed. I did some dishes, folded some clothes, then started unboxing some of their Christmas decorations, including their faux tree. I wanted to surprise them by having their house decorated for when they arrived home since the holidays were only a few weeks away.

Squatting next to a box I was rummaging through, I felt it again. It was stronger than the day before. The presence of a very tall entity standing at my back, exuding such hatred that it made my temples ache. I turned, but the room was empty.

Forcing myself to ignore it and finish my task, I went back to sifting through the box. A minute or so went by, and there it was again. Hatred and malice directed at me. The air was growing slightly colder, and the atmosphere was turning heavy. I turned again, but still, there was no one in sight.

At this point, I decided to abandon the Christmas decorations and just get out of the house for a bit. So, I grabbed my purse and ran some errands to clear my mind.

A few hours later, I was back at the house, hanging some stockings on the mantle. Out of the corner of my eye, I saw what looked like a white mist coming from behind my right shoulder. Immediately, the lights in the living room flickered, and the room turned cold. That's when I realized the mist looked like breath. But spirits didn't breathe, did they? How could they without a human form?

Frozen in place, it felt like someone had placed a dense wall directly behind me like suddenly I was standing right in front of something solid.

That's when pieces of my hair, only on my right side, began to move in an invisible breeze.

I snapped out of the shock of the situation and turned around to find nothing there. It felt like someone had been standing directly behind me, breathing into my ear. It gave me the chills.

I'm not sure who or what lived there before my sister; her house really isn't that old. But there's something malicious there, and it loves to taunt people. I won't set another foot in her house. I refuse.

I didn't even finish house-sitting for her either. After that night, I was out of there.

17 By accident

Some say four in the morning is the "witching hour." The time when there can be the most paranormal activity. A softness in the space in the dimensions of life and death. How uncanny of it, then, to begin at four in the morning for me.

I was in the laundry room, moving some clothes over before heading out to work. Being as I am a nurse in the emergency room at a local hospital, I was trying to get some chores done before I left, so when I got home, I could just take a nap.

After I'd moved the clothes over to the dryer, I noticed something out of the corner of my eye, standing in the middle of the kitchen. It was a tall, opaque shadow of a man. I shook my head in disbelief and began to walk towards him, and then poof, he was gone.

When I arrived at work, I recounted what had happened that morning to a co-worker, Arielle, who believed in such things. She advised me to cleanse our apartment by burning sage. I assured her that at the first opportunity, I would buy some sage and cleanse my apartment.

After burning some sage and purifying our place, nothing else happened for months. However, the air in the apartment felt different. It felt stuffy all the time, and opening the windows didn't help. I thought surely if I got some fresh air inside it would feel better, but it just didn't.

One evening, when I was working earlier than usual, at midnight, I took a lunch break with Arielle. We were sitting out in my van, eating some fast food when she started to ask about the shadow man. I told her I hadn't seen him since I used the sage, but the air in the place still felt heavy.

At that moment, I saw something odd in my side mirror. It looked like the shadow man, but he was standing way back by the main road. Arielle followed my gaze to the mirror and saw it too!

We both watched, curious as to what, if anything, he would do. As if he noticed us watching, he started to glide off down the street, and then two vehicles collided, right there. Metal tore, parts flew, there was the sound of grinding and screeching. My eyes were bulging out in horror.

Arielle was first to get out of the van and run towards the road, while it took me a few seconds longer to get my body to respond. For the entire jog over to the accident, I couldn't help but wonder if the shadow man had something to do with it. Had he caused it? Or was he like death? Was he there to collect someone? And if so, why had he been in my apartment! Was I going to die next?

We reached the accident and dialed nine one one. It was quite the night. We gave first aid until hospital responders arrived and took the victims away. Two teenage girls in one car had run a stop sign, and there was a single male in the other. Both girls were put in the ICU for multiple days, and by the third day, one passed away. The man had minor cuts and some whiplash but was released the same night.

Arielle and I talk about that night sometimes; I think just trying sometimes to make sense of it. Like maybe time would give us some perspective and answers. But we still have no idea what happened that night with the shadow man. At least I was not the only one who saw it. That gave me slight relief.

As for my apartment, I have never seen the shadow being again. I've looked for him, trust me. I have anxiety that he will show up, and something tragic will happen again, but that was nearly five years ago, and so far, he hasn't.

18 The rattler

If you had asked me ten years ago if I thought I would be telling this story right now, I would have said, "No. I do not believe in the paranormal. It's silly, made-up stories by bored people." But then, when I turned sixteen, my world was turned upside down.

One night, around one in the morning, I heard the sound of rattling coming from the kitchen. I sat bolt upright in bed, squinted through the darkness towards the hallway, and listened on high alert. *Reeeeeeikkkk. Reeeeeeikkkk.* There it was again; like chains scraping against the floor or being dragged around.

My heart pounded, and my thoughts raced. "Should I investigate? Should I lay down? Maybe this is all in my head." I slowly sunk back into my bed, pulled the covers up to just below my chin, and decided to listen for a little longer in the hopes that someone was just up late rummaging for a snack or a glass of water.

Seconds ticked by, which felt like minutes. Then, came this awful feeling. It was as if I was blanketed in heaviness. It started at my feet until it shrouded my entire body, and I was unable to move. Terror seeped through my veins like ice shards, and I peered down at my hand and begged it to shift. It would not. I opened my mouth to scream only to realize my mouth wasn't open, and the scream was inaudible and clogged in my throat.

While terrified of the sudden paralysis, I had not noticed that the jangling sound was gaining on me. The sound of something dragging and scraping against the wall in the hall outside my bedroom directed my attention from my frozen limbs to entirely focus on the noise. I silently gulped down my panic and waited for whatever was coming to find me.

From out of the hallway, a black figure ducked inside my room, swaying slightly as it glided closer and closer. Reaching its target, me, it wavered at the side of my bed. Static electricity radiated from it, and although paralyzed, I could feel the tingle that it emitted over my exposed face. I could even feel strands of my hair lifting away from my scalp.

I stared at it in obvious horror out of the corner of my eyes. I felt fresh tears sting my open eyes, and once again, I begged my body to respond, but it still refused. I decided to do the only thing I could do. In my head, I started praying. I prayed probably the hardest I ever have in my life. Then, before the shadow could advance on me further, it dissolved.

With the dissolution came feeling, all of my feeling. Like a superhero springing into action, I leaped to my feet and flipped my bedside lamp on. Looking down, my hands were trembling, I was drenched in sweat, and my heart felt like it would burst right out of my chest at any moment.

For the remainder of the night, I lay awake, occasionally pausing my television to listen for any unusual sounds, but the house remained quiet. Eventually, as the sun began to light up the sky, my anxiety eased, and I finally fell asleep.

Two weeks later, my best friend spent the night, and around midnight, we delighted in making each other giggle by telling ghost stories. Mostly silly tales that were utterly absurd.

Shortly after we'd fallen asleep, I woke to her violently shaking me. I blinked my eyes open, trying to focus on the sudden brightness in the room. Doing my best to pay attention, I listened as she recounted the previous few minutes.

Everything she said matched exactly what had happened to me weeks prior. I couldn't help my bulging eyes and the heaviness in my chest that began to rise to my throat. After the weeks that had passed, I was hoping maybe it had been some horrid dream that had felt real, but after listening to

Lindsey, I knew that the paralysis and the shadow man were real.

Lindsey begged me to call her parents and have them take her home, which I completely understood. After she left, I did not sleep at all. It was another all-nighter for me with all the lights on… listening and waiting. But, like before, nothing reoccurred the same night.

This has been happening to me for over six months now. Sometimes it will be a few weeks before the shadow comes, and sometimes I'll be lucky, and it will wait a month.

I tried to tell my parents what has been happening, but they just reply with, "It was just a bad dream." I know full well, after several repetitions, and what happened to Lindsey, that it is not a dream. It is real, and I fear that unless we move and my parents believe me, it will never leave me alone.

19 Soul shadow

A few friends and I went to a local cemetery, trying to catch some EVP recordings of ghosts. This was our second time doing this, and because nothing bad had happened after the first journey, I was excited when we got to do it again.

Charlotte, my best friend of ten years, and her boyfriend, John, were there; also myself and my boyfriend, Sean. Sean and John went off by themselves over towards a mausoleum. Charlotte and I walked side by side, looking at the ages on the graves while the recorder was switched on.

We stopped once we saw a grave that was from the late eighteen-hundreds. We were chatting away about how that must be the oldest grave we'd seen there so far and such. Then, from behind us, we heard the sound of footsteps in the grass. We turned and looked over our shoulders in unison, assuming it was our boyfriends, but there was nothing there.

A little spooked, we shrugged it off as maybe the wind and kept examining gravestones and markers. Once we'd felt like we had recorded long enough, we packed up our stuff and left with nothing else occurring.

Once home, I told Sean what had happened at the cemetery, and of course, he told me it was our imagination. We were just creeping ourselves out, he'd said, rolling his eyes. That frustrated me quite a bit.

A couple of days later, Sean was taking a shower, and I was watching television in the living room. Suddenly I heard him shriek and yell my name. I burst off the couch, sprinted down the hallway and threw open the bathroom door to find him sitting on the floor in front of the vanity.

"What the heck are you doing?" I'd asked him after scanning the room and finding nothing out of the ordinary.

"There was someone in the mirror," He pointed a finger up behind his head but refused to look in the direction he was pointing. I thought that odd; aren't grown men supposed to be tough?

I sighed and leaned my hands on the vanity, and did a thorough inspection of the mirror. There was nothing unusual in or around the mirror. I'd even checked my reflection. It was me, smiling back.

"You are being silly," I held a hand out to him and forced him to his feet. "See?"

At first, he refused to look into the mirror, so I brought a hand below his chin and tilted it upwards until his eyes met the mirror.

"Ya, I guess you're right," he mumbled, tucking his towel in and walking past me out of the bathroom to our bedroom.

For moments I stayed behind, mostly curious as to what he could have seen. I decided to examine the entire bathroom, but again I came up empty-handed. I guess if I wanted answers, I'd have to ask Sean exactly what he had seen.

Sean was on edge most of the night, so I thought it best to wait until breakfast before inquiring about the mirror. He explained that he had seen a shadow figure in it standing right behind him with an outstretched arm as if he were about to touch him. So, he just dropped to the ground and shrieked out for me to come. His story gave me goosebumps.

Before leaving for work, I purposely went back into our bathroom, shut the door, and stood there for five minutes, daring whatever it was to show itself to me, but it did not. So, I turned the light off, exited the bathroom, and went to work feeling defeated.

When I came home from work, Sean was sitting on the sofa watching something on television. I grabbed a bottle of water out of the fridge and joined him on the couch. We cuddled and watched television until about six when we decided to order a pizza for dinner.

The doorbell rang thirty minutes later, and I hopped up and answered it. Sean watched over the back of the couch while I joked with the delivery guy a bit before shutting the door. As I walked the pizza back over to the couch, I noticed a weird look on Sean's face.

"What's wrong?" I asked as I set the pizza down and opened the steaming box.

"There's someone behind you." His eyes were full of twisted fear, and his skin had turned ghostly pale.

With my heart racing like crazy, I slowly turned and peered over my shoulder, only to see an empty kitchen. I turned back towards him and arched a brow in his direction. "Are you trying to scare me?"

"No." This time it was a whisper, and he was slowly scooting backward on the couch, closer to the wall, as if something was going to get him.

"Sean!" I pounded my fist on the table, annoyed, "This isn't funny. Stop it!" Angrily I sat down and grabbed a piece of steamy pizza from the box and shoved it into my mouth, trying to ignore his stupid charade.

"Becca," He whispered again.

This time I whipped my head towards him, my ponytail bouncing furiously and gave him a nasty look that could cut glass. "What, Sean," I rudely retorted.

"It's still behind you."

I took a deep, annoyed breath and again turned and looked over my shoulder to glimpse nothing at all. "You are starting to piss me off."

His voice changed from scared and helpless to demanding and urgent, "It's right there!" He pointed, shaking his finger over and over. "Why can't you see it?"

I shrugged, grabbed another slice of pizza, and a paper plate, "I don't know Sean," then I headed for our bedroom, "Probably because there's nothing there!" And slammed the door behind me and ate in silence.

Was I scared at this point? Not really. You can't really be terrified of something you cannot see. However, Sean was acting pretty believably, and it was slightly freaking me out. If there was something in our house I could not see, why was it there? We'd lived there for a few years, and nothing like this had happened before. I shook my head in silent thought; this was all really confusing. Was Sean going crazy?

I turned the television on in the bedroom, and then I heard the front door slam in the distance. Obviously, Sean had left. Maybe that would be good for him; some fresh air might help him relax a bit.

The next morning was tense. Sean would hardly look me in the eye or talk to me. I apologized for not believing him, but that did not seem to help. He was highly on edge and had terrible bags under his eyes. I assumed he must not have slept well last night. Maybe he did see something. Should we look for answers?

I asked him to describe exactly what he had seen and pulled out my laptop. I typed it into the search bar and scoured the internet and its images. Sean pointed at the screen when I brought up a photo of what was called "The Hat Man."

Thousands of people, if not more, had recollected either encountering this being or, at the very least, seeing it. Often it happened during sleep paralysis. That was not Sean's case; however, because these events had happened while we were both fully awake.

After picking the picture out, he brought a hand up and ruffled the back of his hair while he paced the kitchen. I drew my face closer to the screen and stared at the entity on the monitor. It definitely was creepy looking. Had that thing really been standing behind me? Eww... I shivered.

Around three-thirty that afternoon, I received a call from my mother. My brother Branson, who had cancer and was home from the hospice, had taken a turn for the worse and I needed to come over immediately. They weren't sure how much time he had left. In their opinion, it could be an hour or maybe one more day.

Sean and I hurried over to Branson's house. For the entire drive, I was lost in thought. Mostly replaying childhood memories in my mind and wishing life had ended up differently for him. He had two young sons, five and twelve, and it just broke my heart that they had to lose their dad so soon.

The crunch of tires on gravel brought me out of my thoughts and back to reality.

"We're here," Sean unlocked the doors and slid out of his side.

I took a long deep breath, grabbed the handle, and got out of the car. I was not ready for this. Not at all. I kept wishing in my head for just one more day, or even a week. A week would be better. I was not ready to say goodbye today.

Inside, my brother laid on the bed with cords and what-not going every which way around him. I kept thinking he must be feeling like a science experiment. How sad. We said our goodbyes and all hovered about him telling funny stories of the life we had all shared with him. Some were quite hilarious!

When it was obvious that he was taking his last breaths, I pushed past family members and sat out in the hallway. Sean followed me. "You okay?"

Tears stung my cheeks, and I hastily wiped them away, sobbing, "No."

He embraced me tightly and rocked me for a while. It didn't make me feel less hurt, but at least he was there for me. I laid my head on his shoulder and closed my eyes, just letting him rock me for a while.

When I opened my eyes, I saw it, The Hat Man. I pulled back from Sean so fast my back bumped against the wall, and I blinked the tears away to clear my vision.

"What the…" Sean followed the direction my outstretched finger was pointing to, and his eyes grew huge. Then he turned to me, "You see him too?"

I nodded, slowly scooting as close to the wall as humanly possible. Sean joined me, and we both just stared up at it. It stood in the doorway to my brother's room, almost as tall as the ceiling. It had no facial features, so I could not tell if it meant harm or good, just that it was standing right in front of me, plain as day.

It was not long before my mom hustled out of the bedroom to check on me, sniffling with tear-stained eyes. As she came through the doorway, she walked right through the shadow man, and he dissipated. Sean and I looked at each other in absolute disbelief and slowly rose to our feet.

I was on edge for the rest of the day, to say the least. It was frustrating because I was overcome with other thoughts when I should have been focusing on my brother's passing and his grieving family.

Nothing else occurred that day, or ever again for that matter. The Hat Man was never seen by us again. It took us a while to accept that, too. We looked over our shoulders for a very long time after that, just waiting for him to come back, but he never did.

Sean and I choose not to talk much about what happened during that time. We are afraid it might bring him back to us or something. But we have both wondered if The Hat Man came because my brother was going to pass. And maybe it was some sort of warning? Or my other theory is whatever it was may have come to take him home. I'm not sure if it is either of these, but it makes it a little bit easier to sleep at night if I put my hope in one of them.

20 Chance

It all started with a trip to the woods. My dog loves fetching sticks and playing in the river, so one summer, I rented a cabin in the woods about fifty miles out of town for the weekend for myself and my dog Chance.

During one of our hikes, we came across what looked like an abandoned shack in a small clearing. Unable to help myself, I investigated the shack. The roof was warping, and the paint was shedding off like flakes of snow. I loved abandoned places; they always intrigued me, so I hung around it for a while. Vines and numerous weeds were starting to invade its small porch, and the windows were thick with years of grime and dirt.

As I was nearing the end of my fascination, Chance began behaving oddly. He backed up slowly as if he'd seen something until his rear end bumped into a tree trunk, and he then just stared ahead at the cottage on high alert. I walked over to him and asked what was wrong, but he ignored me completely, eyes still locked straight ahead.

Finally, I decided it was time to go, and started to walk off in the direction in which we had come from. I called his name and snapped my fingers, and he eagerly joined me, occasionally looking back behind him on our journey back to the cabin.

The next day was our last day at the cabin before packing up and heading home. So, I took Chance to the river and was throwing sticks for him to fetch. He was enjoying himself a little too much, to say the least. His tongue hung out of the side of his mouth, and his lips slightly curved in a satisfied smile every time he dropped the stick at my feet and begged for more.

I threw the stick over my head into the river again and waited for Chance to retrieve it. He galloped into the water at full speed, sending water crashing on both sides of him as he doggy paddled out towards the wood.

In an interesting turn of events, he did not fetch the stick. He shot me a nervous look with wide eyes and refused to grab it. I called to him and pointed at the stick, saying, "Chance, get the stick!"

He just paddled in the same spot as if frozen and unable to gain on it. I scratched my head. What on earth was up with my dog?

Chance seemed to be occupied by something ahead of the stick on the other sand bar. I walked out a bit from where I stood, going around some trees to get a better look, as I shielded my eyes from the sun so I could see better, and then… my breath caught in my throat.

Standing on the sand bar was a shadow of a man. A tall man. If I had to guess, I'd say almost seven feet tall. He had no facial features but one. Glowing deep crimson eyes and they were staring right at Chance.

In shock, and confused that I was actually even seeing this, I called Chance to come back to me, which he did not. Eventually, I found myself wading into the river to retrieve my frozen dog. He clung to me like his life depended on my safety, and he looked over my shoulder at the sand bar as I trudged through the water back to shore.

That was our first encounter with the shadow. Somehow, I had shrugged it off as something we daydreamed. And then the part of me that wanted to question if it actually *was* real, was satisfied that when I assumed if it was, it must be confined to the cabin we were at and once we'd left, it wouldn't be able to follow. I soon would realize that nothing confined this entity to that cabin, and it was free to follow however it wished.

After a few days of being back in familiarity, I had completely forgotten about the odd experience on our short-lived trip. That is until my dog began acting strangely again.

I was sitting in my front room, working on a website design when he started barking from upstairs, which was followed by thumping and yelping and a thundering crash. I quickly shut my laptop, looked over my shoulder at the base of the stairs, and saw Chance trying to collect himself after his fall.

"You okay, buddy?" I walked over to him and leaned down to rub his head. I lifted his paws and checked his arms and legs for any breaks. He seemed fine, just a bit shaken. Suddenly, he began to growl again, a growl I hadn't heard before. It was low and menacing and seemed to come from deeper in his throat than ever before.

Chance's body began to tremble, and I followed his gaze to see where he was looking. The stairs were empty, so for a moment, I sighed in relief… until my gaze met the top landing of the stairs. There was the shadow man. Those blood-red eyes focused on both of us. Chance and I both stood frozen just watching it, waiting for it to do something, anything sinister. Instead, it turned and glided right into the wall beside it and disappeared.

I looked at Chance with what I'm sure was a look of horror and disbelief. While Chance looked at me with his features saying, "What the heck is going on?"

The next weekend I had gone to bed very late. I usually tried to be asleep by midnight, but I'd had a project that I was trying to finish up, and it needed some extra time. I'd put myself to bed around three in the morning only to be awoken around four by something incredibly terrifying.

My bed shook following a heavy pounce, and I sat straight up in the darkness, searching for a culprit. Chance slowly scooted up to me and nudged his head under my arm before looking at me with pleading eyes. Half asleep, I blinked my eyes, trying to focus on the room and my new sleeping buddy. "You know you aren't allowed on the bed," I scolded him.

Following a low whine, he began trembling under my arm. I stroked his head. "It's okay, buddy. What's wrong?"

The sound of something dragging brought my attention from my terrified mutt to the doorway, where there stood a shadow. *The* shadow. The red eyes were glowing exceptionally well through the darkness, maybe more than ever before. I pulled back in shock and scooted closer to the headboard, taking Chance with me.

For only a few moments, it lingered, then its eyes slowly dimmed out, followed by its body, and then it was gone.

By this time, I'd had it. We had not been having these things happening long, but I was up for considering selling my house. I couldn't handle the constant terror anymore. So, first thing the next morning, I started doing a market analysis.

Once I was satisfied with the results of my search, I went to take a shower. In the midst of washing my hair, I heard clattering from the kitchen. I washed as quickly as possible and got out to investigate.

Chance was backed into a corner in my kitchen next to the fridge and standing maybe two feet in front of him was the shadow. He was turned facing my dog. Once I'd come close enough to the shadow, he slowly turned, and his gleaming red eyes bore into mine. This was the first time I'd noticed the shadow take an interest in me. Mostly, he had been pre-occupied with my dog.

With my heart pounding, I mustered the courage to ascend on the entity, but before I could reach him, he disappeared.

My house was on the market within the month and sold rather quickly. I know selling my home wouldn't rid me of the shadow, or at least I wasn't sure. But so far, it's been two years, and we have not seen him since. Maybe he decided to stay in the house and haunt whoever moved in after us, or maybe he went back to the woods where I think he originated.

I know that I learned a valuable lesson from my encounters. Some abandoned places look magical with the overgrowth of nature. Some are intriguing due to the history and the stories they could behold. Others are sinister and are abandoned for a reason. I am no longer entranced by abandoned places; in fact, I'm terrified of them.

21 Armoire

I have acquired myself what I guess you could call a 'follower'. Nearly every day, he is somewhere following me. It comes to me as the appearance of a shadow man, but I get the feeling when he's around that he is more like a demon who has somehow leached on to me.

At first, it began with little things. Something out of place, a drawer I could swear I closed but was open, or a room where I'd turned lights on, but they were now off. Mostly instances you could shrug off as you got busy, and it must have just slipped your mind.

Next came the hair-raising happenings. These originated with low sounds of scratching outside my door at night. Then scraping like there were mice in the walls, burrowed way down deep inside. Or other sounds would be floorboards that never creaked before. Now they'd groan and ache in utter misery in the middle of the night. Audible enough to tear you from a deep sleep.

Then came the presence. Whatever it was, did not show itself right away. It was only the feeling of it. I could feel my sheets indent in the middle of the night as if something sat down next to my legs on the bed, but nothing would be there. Or I could feel breath on my neck as cold as ice throughout the house during the day or at night, followed by a light sigh. One other occasion, I was folding laundry but had the dryer door open since there were a few more articles of clothing inside to fold. I'd reached out my hand to grab more out, and the door slammed shut, barely missing my fingertips.

At one point, I confided in my mom about the happenings, pretty positive that she would react by thinking

I was crazy. She was very sympathetic and talked to me about options on cleansing the house, and just as we had finished our conversation, I happened to glance out of the corner of my eye to see something move in the kitchen. There was a shadow standing by our bar staring at me with glowing white eyes. I tapped my mom's shoulder, unable to speak from shock and pointed.

Following my finger, she asked, "What are you pointing at?"

Because the entity was nearly six feet in height and hard to miss, I took it as she could not see what I was seeing. Also, due to the crazy conversation we had just had, I felt it best not to mention it. I felt I was already pushing the bounds of her acceptance.

After that day, I saw him often. He was always standing in the corner watching me while I watched tv. Or I saw him outside my bedroom window watching me while I did my homework. A few times, he stood in my doorway watching me at night, that is until I got smart and started shutting my door.

I racked my brain for answers. Why had this suddenly occurred? What was different from before until the activity started? Then it hit me like a ton of bricks—the estate sale. Months before, I'd seen this really old armoire at an estate sale. Its features were elaborate and beautiful. I had to have it. Mostly I bought it for college. I was about to graduate and thought it would be perfect for storing my clothes in a new apartment.

I did go back to the house I'd bought it from seeking answers. I was lucky, the house hadn't sold as of yet, and they were still actively doing repairs on it. I spoke with the son of the woman who had passed. His mother had committed suicide after numerous stays in and out of hospitals. She had been bipolar and schizophrenic and was deeply into the occult and practiced witchcraft. That was all I'd needed to hear.

I went straight home, unpacked my things from the armoire, and took it to the dump. I hope it stays there, and someone doesn't try to rehome it as it is in amazing condition. I'm positive something his mother did in her house, or rather something she unleashed had attached itself to that thing and began its torment on me.

I'm in my junior year of college, and I've never seen a shadow figure again since ridding of that thing. I never believed in curses before, let alone demons, but if you asked me, that armoire is cursed by the devil.

22 It's only a photo

My dad and I regularly played tricks on each other. We were the biggest jokers of our family.

One morning, I missed the bus to school. I was walking down the stairs and I could have sworn I saw my dad walk from the kitchen into his office.

When I got to the bottom of the stairs, I went in to my dad's office to ask him for a ride to school. Just as I opened the door about three inches, the door slammed shut in my face. This was followed by the sounds of books falling or being thrown off of his bookcase.

My dad had a stressful job, so I thought maybe he just had something frustrating happen and he was taking it out on the books in his office.

I was still standing right in front of my dad's office door when he came up behind me and sighed loudly. "Did you miss the bus again?"

I turned around and he was standing there with his hands on his hips, dressed fully for work.

I gave him a quizzical look, nodded and went to the kitchen to grab my backpack off of the counter. I kept thinking that my eyes must have played tricks on me. But then, why did the office door slam shut in my face if no one was in there? And who was throwing books around in dad's office?

Fast forward a few years. I believe I was about fifteen at the time. My girlfriend and I were doing homework up in my room. Out of nowhere, my girlfriend pointed at my closet and said, "Did you see that?"

I rolled my eyes, thinking she was being ridiculous. She kept insisting that she saw something over by my closet door, so she snapped a couple pictures of it with her cell phone.

I was laughing and making fun of her the whole time--until we started flipping through them. Then I get goosebumps and chills ran through my veins.

In each picture, we could see a blurry outline of a girl with only half of a face. We high tailed it out of my room and waited downstairs on the sofa for my parents to get home from work.

About a year later, my best friend Brian and I were talking about the time my girlfriend and I took pictures of my closet. He suggested we take some all over the house because he didn't believe me at all.

So, we started downstairs and we thought we saw a couple orbs in some of the pictures. But frankly, we are too novice to decipher if they were actually orbs or dust.

Still not satisfied that we'd captured any proof, he began to tease me. I turned to him and told him about the time I thought my dad went into his office, but he was actually right behind me. So, he suggested we take a bunch of photos in my dad's office.

Just as we opened the office door and snapped two or three photos, we heard a thump on the stairs behind us. We both turned and started shooting pictures of the stairs.

When we checked what we captured, we were both speechless. He captured a tall man with a hat that was like a shadow figure. He was all black but with two glowing eyes. I captured the girl we saw in my bedroom and she was standing right in front of us at the foot of the stairs. I got so freaked out that I made him stand outside with me so I could calm down.

We only lived in that house for about another year or so. But after what I saw in those pictures, I refused to take any more in the house. I felt like not knowing was better than knowing.

23 Deep shadows

I had invited my friend over for dinner and a movie. I was about eighteen years old and still lived with my parents whom Carson had never met before.

We were both lying on my bed watching some YouTube funny blooper videos and out of the corner of my eye, I kept noticing Carson briefly staring at the doorway.

"What do you keep looking at?" I paused the video and turned on my side to face him.

At that moment, you could hear the front door open, keys jangle and footsteps.

I swear all the color drained from his face. "Is that your parents?"

I gave him a questioning look, hopped off the bed and peered over the banister as my mom placed the keys on the table and smiled up at me. "Hi honey!"

I turned back to my room and Carson, "Yup. My mom just got home."

He started trembling, as he explained that he thought he saw my mom walking back and forth from one side of the hallway to the other multiple times in the last hour. Obviously, that was impossible since she had not even been home yet.

About four months later, Carson and I had decided to start dating and again he was over at my house. This is the first time he had been over since the woman he had seen supposedly in the hallway.

I had an essay due the next day and while my parents cooked dinner, I was finishing it in my room. Carson sat at the foot of my bed watching t.v. with the volume fairly low so I could concentrate.

I was sitting at my desk, typing away with my back to the doorway.

Suddenly, I heard him whisper, "Hey Suz, turn around."

I peered over my shoulder at him, mildly annoyed, and then at the doorway. It looked like there was a shadow cast against the wall. It was as if someone were standing in my doorway, projecting their shadow on the wall right behind, except no one was standing there.

To get a better look, I swiveled my chair around to face the doorway completely. In the time it took to whip around all the way, the shadow just seemed to combust and disappear. It was the strangest thing. It didn't just fade away. It's like it closed in on itself.

A few months later, a few of my friends and I were having a sleepover on the floor in my room. It was two of my guy friends and one of my girlfriends. Of course, Carson was one of them.

At some point, Carson and I left to go pop some popcorn in the microwave downstairs. When it was done, we were walking up the stairs side by side, giggling about something that I don't really remember.

We paused in the hall, talking outside my door and I looked to the left of us to the wall. I saw our shadows, but it looked like there was a third in between ours. I nudged Carson's arm so that he would look too.

Just as he saw it, it started moving. It grew about a foot taller than our shadows and glided along the hall all the way to the bathroom at the end and seemed to disappear into it.

We bolted into my room and shut the door behind us.

I have never heard voices in the house or anything more than mostly shadows. It seems like the house is a hot spot for shadowy figures. I have encountered many in all shapes and sizes.

24 Mistakenly haunted

After about a year of dating, I asked my girlfriend to move in. I must note that up until she moved in, nothing notable had ever happened in my apartment. But once she did, whatever it was definitely let us know that it did not approve.

A few days after she moved in, we were having breakfast at the counter. I was getting ready for work and she was getting ready for school. She worked as a teacher's aide until she graduated.

Talking amongst ourselves, we watched as the orange juice bottle suddenly wobbled on the counter. That was the beginning.

Over the next month, both of our laptops suddenly died. They wouldn't even turn on. I took them to a computer repair shop, and they couldn't fix them either. It was highly frustrating.

Then the television in the living room stopped working, so I had to borrow one from my mom. Then, my cell phone battery was draining excessively. I would charge it all night and it would be at one hundred percent, but if I stayed home my battery would be dead in an hour. If I went to work, my battery lasted until I got home. I thought that was really odd.

I was in the living room watching my borrowed t.v., while my girlfriend graded papers for class in the bedroom. After about an hour, she peeked her head out and told me she was taking a break to take a bath.

Apparently, while I was watching television, a black mass formed by the door in the bathroom, hovered near the sink for a minute or two and then just disappeared.

She ran out of the bathroom half wrapped in a towel and really shaken. I was able to get her calmed down and stayed in the room with her while she got some pajamas on.

She decided to bring the papers with her out to the living room to finish grading while I watched t.v. As she shuffled them together and started to grade, she gasped loudly. I paused the t.v. and looked over at her, slightly annoyed.

Holding the papers up for me to see she pointed at the B+. I nodded and said, "Ok and?"

Her eyes widened, "Look at the plus."

I leaned over closer and looked at it. "That's a plus alright," I said trying to joke around.

She was getting a little miffed. "Look closer at the horizontal line."

I rolled my eyes and squinted in the terrible lighting. I wasn't sure what I was even looking for. Isn't a plus a plus?

"I wrote a B minus on there. Something changed it to a plus. The line is jagged and wobbly." She thrust the papers even closer to my face, "LOOK!"

Frustrated, I turned the table lamp next to me on, grabbed the papers from her hand and looked closer. I could tell what she meant. The line was weirdly etched on there. You could tell the pressure she used to write the B- was not the same pressure used to make the horizontal line.

I will admit, it was strange. Fortunately, after a few more months the activity seemed to die down quite a bit. Only a few odd noises here and there remain. No more masses have been seen or any other objects moving or writing on their own.

I honestly don't know what made the difference. Maybe if something was in my apartment, it just took a little while to warm up to my girlfriend and now, they are ok with her being there.

25 Voices

As long as I can remember, I've been sensitive to the paranormal. Most prominently, seeing shadows or hearing voices. On a constant basis, I would hear someone call out my name in a voice that was similar to my mother's, but when I'd go ask what she wanted, she'd say she'd never called for me.

One summer, my best friend had stayed the night with me. We were both sitting on my bed, laughing at videos we were watching on our phones. Then there was my name being called. We both heard it. As I'd done before, I went into the kitchen and asked what she needed, but she had no idea what I was talking about.

I'd gone back to my room confused and told my friend that my mother had never called for me, and it freaked her out. To be fair, I was quite on edge myself. However, this happened so frequently I was starting to get used to it and blamed it on my hearing.

Tragically I lost my father the following summer, and we were forced to move into my aunt's house. That's when the shadows came to life. Terrifying shadows that would stay just long enough for a glimpse then vanish into a wall or darkness.

My Aunt June, my mom and I were sitting at the breakfast table on a Saturday morning. I remember this because it was not a school day. We'd just finished a late breakfast, and it was about ten in the morning when out of nowhere, a few upper kitchen cupboards slowly creaked open by themselves then slammed shut. All three of us witnessed it. We dumbly stared at each other around the table as if our worried glances would generate some answers.

The next spring, I decided to learn to play the piano. My aunt had a huge one, and it was just collecting dust. So, after begging my mom to get me some lessons, she relented. My teacher would come to my aunt's house every Thursday and give me an hour's lesson before dinner.

On this particular day, I was squinting trying to read the sheet music while my teacher sat to my right. She was a middle-aged woman with long brown hair and adorned her fair share of patience. Behind us, we heard a noise from the kitchen. It sounded like someone tripping over a watering can.

We both whipped around to see a greyish shadow gliding from the kitchen into a nearby wall. Exchanging worried glances, we gazed back at the spot, but whatever it was went into the wall and never reappeared. No words were spoken about it, so it's safe to say we made a silent pact to disregard the occurrence.

The shadows and voices stopped for a number of years after that. Life seemed to be a semblance of 'normal' again. Until I moved in with my boyfriend in my freshman year of college, that is.

I had just returned home after school and had set my keys and my purse down on the counter in the kitchen, thinking about making myself a snack. "Julie…."

I turned to the sound of my name. It sounded exactly like my boyfriend had spoken it. I searched the entire apartment for him to no avail. He was not there. I shook my head in confusion and went back into the kitchen to make my snack.

One day after school, I'd come home a little earlier than Dean, my boyfriend. I was in our room doing some research for an essay I had to write by the following day when I heard what sounded like a sigh from the other side of my door.

I quit typing on my computer and listened. I didn't hear anything else, but I did see something. From under the door, you could see what looked like the shadow of feet walking by my door. I assumed Dean was home, so I went out in the hallway to greet him.

Only, Dean was nowhere in the house, and after inspection, his car wasn't even in his parking spot. That gave me the creeps. It's one thing to think your name is being called. You can blame that on your hearing. But the appearance of someone walking in the hallway when no one is home…how do you justify that with an answer?

After graduation, many years later, I was interning at a local hospital. They gave all the crappy shifts to interns, so it was nearly the middle of the night, and I was living on little to no sleep as it was.

I was standing at the nurse's station reviewing a chart with a fellow intern when out of the corner of my eye, I saw a shadow figure duck into room 121. As far as I knew, that room was unoccupied, since the old woman who had been in that room passed away yesterday.

Curious, I pressed down the hall and into room 121. The bed was neatly made, and nothing seemed disturbed what-so-ever. I turned slowly towards the bathroom and, for a split second, glimpsed a shadow figure of a woman staring towards the bed. Before I could notate any features or age, she was gone.

I was dumbfounded. Did I just see a ghost? It was more of a shadow than an actual ghost, though. From what I could tell from the quick look I did manage to get, it was more dark than transparent, and its features were well hidden in darkness.

Regardless of what I did or didn't see, I shrugged it off as too little sleep and too many long, demanding work hours.

Through the years, this hasn't been the only encounter with shadow people I've had, and I'm pretty sure it won't be the last. A lot of people die in hospitals. There is so much energy built up inside there that sometimes it's overwhelming. Hospitals can be truly creepy if you are willing to see what it has to offer.

On average, I see at least one shadow a month, sometimes two. They come as dark beings, transparent entities, and some are just a quick dart in the corner of your eye.

My latest experience was after a little girl with cancer passed away. She was one of my favorite patients. I would read to her for half an hour a day and spoil her with extras from the kitchen whenever I had the extra time to grab some. Jess is what her parents called her, short for Jessica, of course.

Jessica had the purest aura about her. Like she was so innocent and sweet, she was bathed in a white light constantly. She knew no fear, she had no ill will towards God; she was determined to be happy until it was her time.

Her parents had shown up when she started to decline, and it really hit me hard like a punch to the gut. I wasn't ready to lose her. Deep down, though, I knew if it was her time, it was her time. When it comes to terminal cancer, there's not a whole lot left you can do.

Again, I'm out by the nurse's station, which is only about eight feet from her room, when I hear the flat line. Tears welled in my eyes, and I was filled with sadness. I took a deep breath and tried to present myself as professional when her parents came out sniffling. Inside, however, my heart was melting.

I gave her mother a huge hug, and she sniffled onto my shoulder. Looking over her shoulder while we embraced, I saw a little girl, more of a silhouette really, walking down the hallway in front of me towards the exit. I pulled back from Jess's mom and leaned to one side to look around her at the shadow.

Once I had it in my view, it was just disappearing through the doors at the exit. My luck has been awful with all of my encounters thus far. I see them just as they disappear before I can make out much of anything but an outline. But if you ask me, I saw Jess walking down that hallway that day. And I'm positive she will not be the last soul I see in our hospital.

26 Terrifying remodel

Hired to do a remodel for a recently purchased home, I was working in the kitchen, starting to pull up the flooring. It was about lunch time and I was thinking about stopping to take a break.

At the front door, there were three loud bangs that almost sounded like heavy knocks, so I put my tools down and went to see who was at the door. No one was there.

Obviously, I thought it odd, but figured that maybe it was kid's playing a prank knowing the house was under construction. After all, the home was the perfect target for a trick.

A few afternoons later, I was in the guest bathroom laying some tile. I heard what sounded like creaking boards from the kitchen, as if someone was walking around in there. Unsure what the noise could possibly be, because the front door did not open, I went to investigate.

No one was in the kitchen, so I proceeded to check the entire house room by room. I came up empty-handed. There was no one in the house but me. I brushed it off and went back to laying tile.

The next morning, I was laying new backsplash in the kitchen. Then I heard a splashing noise coming from the guest bathroom. I stopped what I was doing and listened closely for a few moments. It sounded as if the sink was on.

At this point, I was swearing under my breath because something was in this dang house and it would not let me finish a job to save my life. I was getting pissed.

I turned off the faucet and decided to leave my cell phone in the bathroom to record and see what I could capture.

Once I was finished with the backsplash, I went to collect my phone and inspect it to see if I caught anything.

In the first part of the video, I saw the lone towel on the sink slowly slink closer and closer to edge and finally fall to the ground. Okay, that was a little weird but not too bad.

Then, I saw what looked like a black mass shadow figure form on the wall and waver for a few minutes before gliding towards the door frame and then just dissipating entirely.

To be honest, I was not shocked. After the last couple of days, I highly suspected that something was in there with me.

Fortunately, I only had one more day of work before I was finally finished with what I was contracted for. I finally got to leave that house and that paranormal mass for good.

27 The collector

I was in the antique business. It was a family-owned business and I was the third generation to run it.

My wife Shelly and I would delight ourselves on the weekends by going to yard sales and garage sales and seeing what treasures we could find. Sometimes we would have a contest who could find the best stuff with five dollars.

Shelly was the best at this. She would always beat me. One time, she did so much smooth talking she got an antique brass rotary phone for a dollar.

Her ability to wheel and deal astonished me to no end.

There was a particular day that Shelly and I went yard sale hunting. We had been out and at it for about two hours when we pulled up to an estate sale. The lawn was lined with cluttered tables. We nearly salivated on our walk from the car. We could see from the street that there were mountains and mountains of treasures begging to be added to our store.

"Oh my gosh Nick!" Shelly exclaimed and held up an Adamantine Mantle Clock. It was in pristine condition for its age. The feet, lion's head and column capitols all had a pleasant bronze finish.

"How much is it?" I called to her without turning my head from the trinkets I was looking at.

"Only $10!"

"Well get it then."

Shelly tucked it under her arm and wandered off to a different table to browse. I kept my focus on the table at hand, mentally running numbers through my mind.

You know you are a good antique seeker if you can mentally remember the value of almost anything. You have to know this. In order to turn a profit, you need to know everything's worth on the spot.

Out of the corner of my eye, my jaw dropped. No way. Sat perched by the front door was a four-piece set of antique English Jacobean chairs. Their resale value would be insane. I hurried over to check the price. Twenty dollars apiece. I scoffed. You've got to be kidding me!

I regrouped with Shelly to pay. We were elated on our finds at this estate sale. We had found nearly twenty things to add to our store and the chairs alone were worth almost one hundred thousand dollars. (I paid eighty for them).

We loaded the car, gave each other a peck and an overjoyed high-five and drove towards the store.

One of the things I love most about my wife is that we share our obsession of antiques. Shelly can see a rusty trinket that everyone else would say "Eww" and know that if it was shined and maintained, it would be gorgeous and expensive. She was my world. We looked out for each other.

Once we unloaded our finds in the garage at the store, Shelly turned to me, holding the clock.

"Can I keep this one? I really like it."

I gave her my squinted, "but you want to keep everything" look. "Fine. But that's the only one!"

She chuckled, "Alright, twist my arm. Only this one then."

After I closed up the shop and had finished logging the new inventory, I investigated the clock. I wanted to check that everything worked. For the price she'd paid, I doubted it worked. I wanted to surprise Shelly and bring it home polished and working fine.

I sat in my chair, magnifying glass up to my eye, and gave it a look-over. Everything seemed in decent condition.

There were a few minor scuffs in the bronze, but nothing I couldn't fix. Then I saw crusty red stuff on the bottom of the clock. It was only the size of a pea. I squinted my eyes and brought the magnifying glass closer. Was that blood?

I shrugged it off. If it were blood, it could have gotten there a million different ways. I cleaned the clock up and fixed the hands. They fired to life. Perfect! Shelly would be so excited.

At home, Shelly was in the kitchen pulling some banana bread from the oven and stirring something on the stove. She hummed to herself as she clicked off the oven.

"Hello honey," she smiled and kissed me.

From behind my back I pulled out the clock and handed it to her, "Something beautiful for my beautiful wife."

She tussled my hair. "Awe, you are the sweetest! You cleaned it up for me. Is it working?"

"I had to mess around with it for a bit, but it seems to be working fine now. What's for dinner?"

"French onion soup and banana bread."

Once dinner was over, we watched a half hour or so of t.v. and then went to bed. Shelly placed the clock on her nightstand on her side of the bed.

At one o'clock in the morning, we awoke to the oddest of noises. It was not quite a knock but a low tapping noise.

Shelly gripped my arm with her shaking hand in the dark. Both of us were on high alert yet disoriented from being half asleep.

Shelly was whimpering. "What is it Nick?"

Forgetting the pitch dark of the room, I rose my finger to my lips to shush her. "Quiet a moment honey."

Through the dark, I saw her head bobble slightly and her whimpers ceased.

I leaned towards Shelly and the tapping seemed to grow louder on her side of the bed. I bent over more to where my body was lightly laying on hers and it was even brasher.

With a quick tug of my hand I turned on the bedside light and the noise concluded. What on earth?

"Did it sound like it was coming from the clock?" I asked rubbing the sleep from my eyes.

Shelly gulped, wide-eyed and nodded. "I think so yes."

"Well what the hell is wrong with the thing? I tinkered with it earlier and it seemed fine." I ran my fingers across my scraggly greying beard in thought.

Shelly just stared at me like a doe mesmerized by headlights, shrugging.

We turned the television on, more for background noise than entertainment. An hour passed before we eventually made our way comfortably tucked back in under the covers.

When the light finally woke me from sleep, I outstretched an arm to an empty spot on the bed. "Shelly!" I called.

"Yes, Nick?" Her voice drifted from downstairs.

"Just checking," I called back.

My old body creaked and groaned every time I needed to get anywhere. Slowly, I managed to get out of the bed and over to my robe hanging on the closet door.

I cocked my head to the side in confusion after fetching my robe. There were scratches on the door. I leaned my groaning body lower to get a better look.

GET OUT. It was written as if a child of six or seven etched it in, but it was as clear as day.

"Hey Shell, come look at this," I bellowed.

Shelly padded up the stairs and stood in the doorway. "What do you need? I'm making pancakes and they are going to burn!"

I waved her to come over. "Look and tell me what this says."

"G-E-T O-U-T. Get out." She gasped. "Who wrote this?"

I gave her a sarcastic glare, "Well how the hell should I know? Does that look like I wrote it?"

"Wow, aren't you quite the bear this morning!" Shelly turned on her heels and was headed back to the kitchen.

What help she was! I continued to investigate the inscription. How odd. Surely, if that had been there before, I would have noticed. I hung my robe there every day.

Finding no real answer, I shook my head, threw my robe on and went down for some burnt pancakes.

After work that day, I fetched the clock and opened that baby up and took a second look at her. Nothing was out of the ordinary and it seemed to be working just fine. Huh….Weird.

I put the clock back together and set it back on the nightstand. Shelly was already in bed and it was only seven.

"Going to bed a little early tonight?"

She nodded. "I'm so tired. I couldn't sleep very well last night."

I plopped my aging body next to hers. "I know exactly what you mean. Business was slow today, so it took forever for the time to go by. I swear I nodded off twice at the shop."

She giggled, "Oh, I believe you. You nod off all the time even when you aren't sleep deprived."

I rolled my eyes and pulled out my book. It was not long before we both drifted off into an early slumber.

One o'clock in the morning came too early for both of us. There was the same scratching noise again.

"Shell, you awake?"

"Ye-yeah." I could feel her trembles through her voice.

"You stay here, I'm going to see if I can find it without turning the light on this time."

She gulped as a reply.

As slowly as my old body would allow, with a few pops of my joints here and there, I got off of the bed and put both feet on the floor. I tip-toed to her side of the bed and listened. It was definitely louder over there.

I got down on my knees and listened before looking under the bed. Nothing was under there either. I was starting to feel like a young boy with monsters hiding in his room.

I rubbed both hands over my face in tired frustration. I just could not seem to figure it out.

"Shell, just turn the light on and stop the noise," I demanded annoyed and defeated.

"Where are you going?"

"I have to pee."

"O-Ok."

In the bathroom I didn't close the door all the way nor did I think to turn a light on. After I was done and washing my hands, I saw it. It was like a pitch-black blob. Like an ink spill that seemed to form into person. Not fully a person, but a shadowy silhouette of a person. Then its eyes glowed at me.

I blinked my eyes repeatedly and then rubbed them. I could not believe what was happening. Then it started to hiss at me. A hiss like the air slowly releasing from a tire.

I quickly slid out the bathroom door and motioned for Shelly to follow me. "Come on, get up!" I harshly whispered.

"What on earth?"

"Something – Is in the b-a-t-h-r-o-o-m."

Those doe in the headlights eyes stared at me again.

"Come on hurry up, go downstairs now."

We sat in the kitchen for what seemed like hours until daylight. We went through two stiff pots of coffee I'm sure.

We talked about the obvious. The Clock. It had to be the clock. I was pretty sure the clock had a demon of some sort attached to it or was haunted. Whatever it was, I did not want it in the house anymore and thankfully Shelly fully agreed with me.

In the light of day, I walked it out to the trash. Good riddance.

Since the clock has been gone, nothing unusual has happened. No tapping or scratching or shadows with eyes.

I guess this is a lesson at best. Sometimes you can find a good deal through other's treasures, but everything has a history. History comes with past's that are unknown.

28 Sisters entity

It all began the summer I went to visit my older sister, Emily, in her new apartment in New York City.

I was barely eighteen and trying to decide what direction to go in with my life. I was an aspiring animator but was trying to find the right college. While deciding, I wanted to stay with my sister in the Big Apple to see if I liked it there.

At the time, she was single but dating. So, some nights she would be home right after work, and others she would meet a guy for drinks or go out with her friends.

On this night, she was out late either having a couple drinks with work friends or trying to meet guys. Honestly, I'm not sure which and I don't think it really matters anyway.

I went to bed around ten-thirty p.m. I always leave the television on for background noise while sleeping because I'm a bit of a scaredy cat when it comes to being home alone.

At midnight, I woke up to a kitten meowing. I thought this was odd since my sister didn't own a cat.

I tiredly grabbed my phone off the nightstand, sat up in bed and turned on the flashlight on my phone. I scanned the room to see if a cat mysteriously had gotten in her apartment. I didn't see anything.

Almost fully awake now, I decided to snap some pictures of the almost dark room with my camera on my phone. Then I started scrolling through them. (I had seen this on ghost t.v. shows.)

In two of the pictures, there was what looked like a black mass of a man standing directly in front of the t.v., possibly holding a cat.

I freaked out! I turned the nightstand lamp on and refused to take any more photos. If something was in there with me, I didn't want to see where it was now.

I stayed up the remainder of the night and fell asleep at first daylight.

A few days later, I was in bed again around ten p.m., but this time my sister was home. She was in the living room with a friend from work, drinking some wine and watching a movie.

It started as a tapping noise on the closet doors. Then it grew a little bit louder. I was sure it was loud enough for them to hear from the living room.

I snapped a few pictures of the closet area and ran out into the living room to flip through them. After last time, I was not doing it alone in my room.

My sister waved at me when I came in the living room. "Couldn't sleep huh?"

I frowned. "I think your apartment is haunted."

They both stared at me like I had just spoken a foreign language.

"Come again?"

"So, the other night while you were out, I snapped these pictures after waking up to what sounded like a cat." I handed her my phone and she scrolled through them.

"No way!" She gasped and handed the phone to her friend, "Dana look. Doesn't that look like a man?"

Dana looked at the phone and gasped as well. "Whoa. That's creepy dude."

I threw my hands in the air in frustration, "Right?!" I sat down next to them on the couch and took my phone back. "Just now, something was tapping in the closet in there and I took some pictures, but I haven't looked at them yet."

They paused their movie and looked over my shoulder at my phone as I scrolled.

"Dude," Dana gasped, "Those look like orbs!"

My sister nodded, "Sure do."

"Has anything weird happened here before I moved in?"

Emily paused and looked up at the ceiling, as if racking her brain. Then, pointing a finger up in the air, she noted, "There was this one time I was in the shower and it sounded like my front door slammed closed. Then, when I got out, I checked the front door and it was still locked. But other than that, no."

"Well, I'm not sleeping in there tonight," I sprawled my legs out on the L shape of the couch. "Looks like I'm out here tonight."

Emily groaned. "Fine. We are almost done anyways."

Again, days passed and not much happened. At this point I must mention that her apartment was on the third floor and there was this huge tree right outside my window.

After a few nights on the couch, I was back in the room, calmed down from the closet incident and ready to try again.

This time, it was about midnight and I was having a harder time falling asleep. Just as I was dozing off, it sounded like someone was throwing pebbles at my window.

I put my head to the glass and cupped my hands around my face to see. I didn't see anything out of the ordinary. I started to pull my hands away from the glass and the tap happened again. It sounded like if the window hadn't been there, a rock would have hit me in the face. It was so creepy!

I whipped out my phone, opened the window and started taking pictures yet again.

I closed and locked the window and flipped through them. I caught what looked like a little boy sitting high up in the tree with a gaping mouth. The freaky thing is that the branches of tree were only about eight feet from the window.

The next morning, I showed my sister the photos. Again, she was horrified.

I decided to pack my bags and head back home for a while. I couldn't live here anymore. I was sleep deprived and honestly getting more terrified by the day of what would happen next.

My sister only lived there for about another year or so. Then, she finally found a boyfriend and they moved in together across town. She still swears that the only thing she had happen was the sound of a door slamming while she was in the shower, even though my phone proved there was much more there than that.

29 Don't wake the baby

Our daughter was born in the fall. For the first little bit, we were living with my mom and dad until our house was finished being built.

Our room was upstairs and little Emma's room was to the right side of ours.

The first odd thing to happen was when my husband Richard and I were in bed talking about politics. (We are both big on that topic and loved to debate with each other.)

I heard Emma sigh while sleeping and it sounded like the monitor moved a little bit. It was hard to describe the sound. It was like the sound of when someone bumps a camera while its on a camera stand.

We both looked over at the monitor and saw what looked like two or maybe three shadow people standing at the foot of her bassinet.

Richard jumped out of bed and went to check on her while I was still staring at the baby cam.

The minute he flipped the lights on, they all disappeared. Like poof, gone. It blew my mind.

I yelled at him to shut the lights off again and he did. Nothing was on the monitor. Odd. Did we see what we thought we saw?

With nothing else happening on the monitor, we brushed it off as our mind playing tricks and went to sleep.

About a month later, in the middle of the night, we were fast asleep. We were jolted from our slumber to what sounded like fists banging on the other side of our wall (Emma's room).

Again, Richard jumped out of bed and ran in there while I hastily grabbed the baby cam and checked it. I saw nothing out of the ordinary. No shadows, nothing.

Richard came back in, shrugging. He hadn't seen anything unusual either.

Fast forward about three months or so. We were about two weeks away from our house being finished. It was the day we did the final walk-through on our home. My mom and dad had flown to Hawaii the day before to celebrate their wedding anniversary, so we had the house to ourselves for a whole week.

Like before, it was bedtime. Richard had already dozed off and was lightly snoring and my eyes were getting tired as well. I was just reaching for the lamp to shut it off when I heard what sounded like two jumps. It was like someone jumped two times in the hallway really hard.

I pulled my hand back and just laid there and listened. I wasn't sure if I'd really heard anything. I was really tired so maybe my mind was messing with me.

Suddenly, I heard footsteps. It was a pounding down the hall, like a sprint headed right for our side of the hallway. I punched Richard in the arm, and he awoke just as the footsteps sounded like they reached our door.

It took everything in me to not scream at the top of my lungs, I was so terrified. Something had just run full force from one end of the hallway to either our door or Emma's.

"What the hell?" Richard squealed. "Why did you punch me?"

"Did you hear it?" I hissed a whisper.

"Hear what?"

"Footsteps. Something ran from the other side of the hall and stopped when it reached our door. Please go check." I gave him a terrified glance.

He sighed and shook his head as he got out of bed and went out into the hallway. Then I heard him open Emma's door and check her room. Nothing.

By the time our house was ready to move into, we were both sleep deprived and eager to get the heck out of my parent's home.

After we moved in, I feared maybe something could have followed us there. We've been in our new home for four years now with nothing otherworldly happening.

30 unholy

My mom recently got re-married, but they hadn't had time to have a formal honeymoon yet. Finally, they were able to do so. Because they had just purchased a new home and were not yet familiar with the area, they asked me to housesit while they went on their vacation. I only lived about thirty minutes from their new place, so I packed my car, grabbed my dog, and drove over there.

Upon entering their home, which was adorned with crown molding, high ceilings, and large bay windows, I did not get a creepy feeling at all. If anything, the house was bright and cheery. But as each night began to draw in, I would start thinking quite differently.

The first night I'd gone to bed in their guest room. My dog, Sophie, a sweet little terrier mix, slept in bed with me. I'd read a book for about fifteen minutes before my eyes became heavy. I placed my book on the nightstand and switched off the light.

I started to dream about the room I was in and could see myself actually sleeping. My arm was hanging off the side of the bed, dangling there. I watched myself snoozing, not being able to tear my attention away. Finally, a blackened, shriveled hand came out from under the bed and began pulling at my hand that hung down. Then the sensation that came with that poured over me. I could feel what I was seeing.

At that same moment, my attention jerked to my body that lay on my back in bed. The comforter began sagging as if something were crawling up my bed towards my chest. Then it reached my chest. My chest indented a little as whatever it was kneeled or sat on it, and then breathlessness took over me, and I was unable to gain breath. It was the most horrible dream I'd ever had.

Finally, I woke, or at least I assumed I did; my eyes were open, and I was in my body, but the feelings of breathlessness and the arm pulling remained. I tried to scream, but nothing came out, and my entire body tingled from paralysis.

With my face turned slightly to the side, I watched my dog sleeping peacefully next to me, completely oblivious to what was happening on the other side of the bed, to me. My eyes watered as if pleading with my dog to sense something was wrong, wake up and bark and end my torment. But yet, she did not.

I felt my lungs, like heavy airless weights, crushing into my spine. My arm felt like it might be pulled right off me from whatever was coming from under the bed. I could feel the vein on my neck pumping in overtime, and its pulse was at an unnatural speed.

I attempted to scream again but to no avail. And then again. Nothing. A third time, and finally a squeak. We were getting somewhere! I mustered all

I could and screamed again, and this time, it was so loud the neighbors must have heard it. The tingling in my body disappeared at the same time, my dog lurched upright and stared at me in horror from the shock of my sudden piercing scream.

Whatever had my arm recoiled and released me, and the pressure on my chest floated away into nothing. I blinked my eyes into the darkness, drew in a deep, heavy breath, and released it as a sigh. I drew my arm back from the side of the bed and draped it over my forehead just trying to make sense, if there could be any, of what just happened.

Sophie, still curious and alarmed, mosied over to my face and licked at my cheek, then nuzzled her body up to my hair.

After laying there for what was probably another hour, I got up from bed, went to the living room and watched some TV. There was no way I was going to be able to sleep the rest of the night for sure. I'd never in my life had something like that happen to me before, and my mind was racing with questions. Had it all been a dream? But It had felt so real.

The next night was, unfortunately, no better than the first. I'd made sure to leave the bedside light on and went to bed around eight. I had been a zombie all day at work and thought if I went to bed earlier, I'd be able to catch up on some much-needed rest.

Again, I was in the guest room, and Sophie was in bed with me, but this time at the foot of the bed, next to my feet. I was flipping through some news on my phone, trying to tire my eyes out, when Sophie began to growl.

I dropped my phone to my chest and watched Sophie at the bottom of the bed. She sat, alert, staring at the bedroom door. In the doorway was a hooded shadow figure. It was mostly pitch black, and due to the light I'd kept on, I could tell it was about seven feet tall.

Another low growl escaped Sophie's throat as the figure appeared to inch slightly forward. I matched it. I inched slightly towards the headboard.

Just like the night before, my heart was pounding at an unhealthy rate.

The shadow stopped at the foot of the bed, not far from Sophie, and she growled in disgust. All of a sudden, her head bobbed down as if something had smacked her, but nothing did. She yelped, jumped off the bed, ran past the shadow, and scurried out into the hallway with her tail between her legs. Now it was just him and me. And I was terrified.

I held my breath and inched up as far as I could without physically climbing the headboard itself. Then the figure just dissolved. I let my breath out in a huge whoosh of relief. Thank God.

But, just as my body began to relax, and my heart slowed down, I felt it. The bed shook slightly from pressure, and the bedding near my feet indented on either side of me. Something was climbing onto the bed—something I could not see.

I sprang off the bed as fast as possible, beelined for the door, and almost running into the door jam. I looked over my shoulder before my exit to see a clearly indented handprint on my pillow, and I was out of there.

I didn't even pack up the stuff I had brought with me. I grabbed my purse and my keys and my dog, got in the car and drove straight home without looking back.

I have never told my mom what happened to me in her house. I'm honestly not sure if she would believe me. But one thing I do know is I will never, ever, ever, go back to that house. Ever.

31 Cursed classic

Before I begin, I am going to say that I was not a believer in the paranormal at all. I thought it was all fiction. Dissuading me from this would have been a hard feat if I hadn't experienced what I am about to tell you first-hand. I now believe in curses and ghosts. What I experienced may have been more of a demon than a ghost, but I am not entirely sure. Regardless, it was the last classic car I ever bought and restored.

Three years ago, I thrived on buying classic cars and restoring them to their former glory. Some, I would keep as trophies, and some I would resell for quite the pretty penny.

I saw an ad online for a 1958, Austin-Healey 100. She was quite the beauty. Sure, she had fallen on some hard times, but with my expertise, I knew restoring her to her previous beauty would be a fun ride. Well, I thought it would be, anyways.

After I'd purchased the car and was driving her home, I was stopped at a red light. I took this opportunity to adjust the side mirror and noticed something odd in it. There were two cars behind me at the light, and just behind the second appeared the shadow of a man just wavering in the street. I blinked my eyes a few times, but there it was on the road, plain as day.

A loud blare of a car horn snapped me back to the road and the light that had turned green, and I continued my drive, a little unnerved. Occasionally, I would glance in the mirror, and everything would be normal; o more shadow.

Nothing happened for a few days. I'd ordered parts for the car, and it would be at least a week before any of them began to arrive, so I just drove her around as she was.

On two more occasions, I saw shadows in the mirror. Once on a sidewalk, and once in the parking lot of a grocery store. You have to realize, for a non-believer, I thought I was going crazy.

Then, the shadows stopped appearing in the mirror; they were closer now. Peeking out behind a shrub in my front yard, or in the hallway of my home, or dodging around a corner. At that point, I didn't feel safe anywhere. Whatever it was had followed me home and let itself right on in.

Finally, the car parts began to arrive, and I'd quit driving the car around town. Instead, I perched her up in my shop and began taking off the old and putting on the new. Whatever it was really didn't like that at all.

A bin of nails up on a shelf fell off and crashed to the floor while I was under the car working one day; scared the daylights out of me. I couldn't figure out how it had fallen. The shelf was thick, and the bin wasn't even close to the edge.

On another occasion, while working on the vehicle, the garage door of my shop started freaking out. It was opening maybe a foot or so then closing again. This happened about ten times until I threw my dirty rag on the floor and exited the shop in defeat.

I couldn't take it anymore. This was already overwhelming. I had no answers for any of this. All I could put together was that something evil was attached to this car.

I put it up for resale online and included the parts I'd bought in the hopes of recouping some of the expenses, which I did. And after it was gone, all the terrifying things ended.

If you ask me that car is cursed. I did look up the history of the car and saw that it had been in an accident at one point. A man was driving up towards the mountains, had lost control on a turn and hit a tree. He'd died on impact. So, was all this tied to the man who had died? Was he unwilling to let anyone make changes to his vehicle?

Or was the car just cursed by something eviler? I'll let you decide.

32 Ghost storage

In 2006 I was a security guard at a storage facility. Evening shifts consisted of me alone during the week and another person on the weekends.

Thanksgiving was just around the corner, and I was slightly preoccupied with the sleeping arrangements in my household. My family was coming into town in a few days, and it was causing a little chaos with my wife.

Around midnight, I was sitting in my chair, halfway kicked back with my feet on the counter and eight monitors in front of my feet. I was flipping through my phone, pricing hotels to see if any were affordable enough to refer my family to. Then, out of the corner of my eye, I saw this black mass skate across one of the screens. I dropped my feet to the floor, scooted my chair closer, and squinted at the video footage, hoping it would repeat itself.

Nothing else happened on the screen, but, unsure of what I'd just seen, I decided to go and investigate. When I got to that exact row of units, I didn't see anything unusual. I shone my flashlight in every nook and cranny to be thorough. Nothing. Shrugging it off, but still with a feeling of unease, I breezed back to the office and sat back in front of the screens.

The rest of that night was uneventful, so I brushed it off as maybe a bug passing by a camera.

Two weeks later, I was again at work by myself. This time I was not preoccupied with anything and paying full attention. Next to unit 126, I saw what looked like a circular shadow on the ground, almost as if someone had dumped water on it so it was darker than the rest. Then, in horror, I saw this blackness rise into the form of an actual person. It was not a ghost but a black silhouette, like a shadow. It turned towards the camera as if it knew I was watching it, wavered in place, then burst into blackness and raced by the screen. I blinked my eyes in disbelief. There's no way that just happened. Yet, after pinching myself to assure myself I was awake, I knew it had.

Nearly a month after the previous event, I was working at the weekend with Chris. I had gone to the bathroom, and while inside, heard her exclaim, "No way!"

When I came out, I asked who she was talking to since it was just the two of us there, and she said she'd seen something I wouldn't believe. I chuckled and told her, "Try me."

She had just seen the same shadow figure I'd been seeing. Same place, in front of unit 126. Apparently, she was more determined than I and had spent the next few days inquiring about unit 126 for answers.

It turns out the owner hadn't paid on their unit and was severely behind to the point of getting locked out of it.

Fast forward another month. Chris got word that the owner had actually died, and that is why it never got paid. So, did the owner leave something in there he was determined not to leave behind, or what? I'm not exactly sure, but that's my guess. He still shows up from time to time. Sometimes every few weeks, and sometimes not for months.

33 The neighbor

It started on a typical Friday night. My parents hired me to babysit my eight-year-old brother, Jon, while they went out for the evening with friends.

I'd ordered pizza and watched TV with him. When 8:30 rolled around, I put him up to bed and sat back on the sofa, flipping through the channels for something to watch.

We have a video doorbell, and my phone, as well as my parents' phones, are linked to it. At 10:13, I received a notification that something had set off the doorbell. I pulled my phone out and went to the app and waited. I didn't see anything odd at all, so I thought a truck, or something, had set it off. I tucked my phone away and continued surfing channels.

When 11:13 came around I was notified of motion at the door again, and I checked my phone. At first, I was dumbfounded. There was nothing unusual. And then, at the tail end of the video was a shadow that came out of the wall from the garage, floated past the door, and behind a tree. I couldn't believe my eyes. I played it back like three times. It was a short shadow, maybe three feet tall. Never have I ever heard or seen anything like it. I was a little spooked, but since it didn't come into the front door or anything, after a while, I pushed it out of my mind.

Around midnight I was in the kitchen making some popcorn because I was hungry. I was texting my boyfriend while waiting for the microwave to ding. Just after receiving a text from him, my phone lit up with motion at the front door again. By this time, my hands were trembling because I wasn't sure I wanted to see what the shadow was doing now.

After standing there frozen, listening to the microwave yell at me that it had completed its task, I finally found the courage to enter the app and watch the footage. This time the shadow was a tad larger, maybe four feet tall. It started by peering around a hedge towards the front door with bright white eyes, then disappeared back behind it. Five seconds before the recording ended, a black mass in the shape of a staticky blob flew from behind the hedge and hovered in front of the camera, then the footage ended.

I was starting to feel on edge, so I went upstairs, checked on Jon, who was soundly asleep and called my boyfriend to keep me company. I told him about the notifications, and he wanted me to send them to him, so I did.

Nearly 20 minutes later, I was notified of motion again, and I was terrified. But this time, the doorbell rang as well. When I pulled up the app, it was my boyfriend. I sighed with relief and let him in. He'd decided, since watching the videos, to come over so I would not be alone.

This happened the entire night until my parents got home. Every hour at 13 minutes past. Exactly.

After this night, it never happened again. However, I think I found some answers the following day. Our neighbor across the street had died that night around 10 pm. He had a heart attack in his house, and they didn't find him until the next morning. I am pretty sure the shadow being was my dead neighbor. Possibly unsure that he was dead? Or maybe trying to figure out where to go after death. I don't know, but I've never seen anything like it in my life, and it still gives me the chills.

34 Johnny

I often travel for work, so I'm used to sleeping in unfamiliar beds in unfamiliar places. I don't usually get anxiety when staying at a hotel that I have never been to before, because like I said, I've been to many.

When I arrived and checked in, I swiftly went to my room to settle in, so I had time for a nice dinner before doing some work prep for the next day's early morning meeting.

Upon entry into my room, the whole space felt stuffy. Like the air mass was off, heavy and disinviting. I tried to shrug it off as maybe the hotel didn't have the best ventilation and continued to unpack my things.

Within a few minutes, I was disturbed by the sound of light footfalls by the door. Not the hallway side of the door, but the inside room side of the door. The hairs on my arms prickled on end and I stood very still trying to listen. It had stopped. Because I didn't hear it again, I brushed it off as I was just unusually jumpy.

Soon I retreated out of my room and enjoyed that wonderful meal I was looking forward to so much. Then I proceeded back to my room, running a checklist through my head on what I needed to cover before bed. I inserted the key in the door, pushed it open briskly, and reached for the light switch. Before I was able to switch it on, however, I stumbled on something large and heavy in my path and fell flat on my face.

Blindly, I reached for the wall, and upon finding it, came to my feet. What could be in my path? I only had one suitcase and a laptop bag, and there had been nothing on the floor earlier. Finally, after groping the wall for a few moments, I uncovered the switch and flipped it on. My suitcase was strewn in my pathway, unzipped and everything.

I furrowed my brow in confusion, but I unpacked it and zipped it up, then put it in the closet. Frustrated and feeling slightly forgetful, I nudged the suitcase against the wall and sat on the edge of the bed, running one hand through my hair.

I just didn't understand it. Had a maid been in my room and pulled my suitcase out? Maids didn't clean late at night, did they? I could find no answers for the odd occurrence, but decided to call the front desk and ask if anyone had been in my room, to which obviously the answer I received was "No."

I cradled the phone back in place and walked over and turned on the air conditioner, which sputtered to life like a classic Ford then gusted a force to reckon against. I felt the cold breeze wash over myself and the room, and for a minute, the air inside seemed slightly less heavy.

I pulled my laptop bag out of the closet and sat on the bed and began to go through some of my work documents. It was not an easy feat. Thoughts kept creeping in my mind about the footsteps and the mysterious placement of my suitcase.

Around midnight I decided to throw the towel in. I abandoned my laptop beside my bed and slid under the covers.

Not too long after sleep took over me, did I wake. At first, I was disoriented because I was in a new bed, but then because the air-conditioner was no longer on, it was off.

I sat up in bed, letting my eyes adjust to the darkness and stared in the direction of the air-conditioner, trying to decide why it had shut itself off. The green light that signaled to me earlier that it was on was now vacantly black.

Just as I was about to discard the covers and turn the infuriating thing back on, I saw it. A black shadow of a man standing only feet from the bed. It was not very tall, maybe five feet, but it sure was unnerving.

I pulled the covers up in defense, and just gawked at the shadow awaiting its intent. The figure did not advance; it just was there. There were no definitive facial features to it, just a mass of blackness.

For a grown man, it takes a lot to make me tremble, but I will admit I was shaking under those sheets.

After what seemed like hours but was merely maybe a minute in real time, the shadow caved in on itself and was gone. I let out a long gust of air I'd been holding and laid there in bed, trying to make sense of it all.

In all my life, I'd never had anything remotely paranormal or unexplained happen to me, so this was quite a new experience. I wasn't sure if I felt like getting in the car and driving straight home, or if I was intrigued by what had just happened. One thing I did know was that the whole experience shocked me.

Needless to say, the rest of the night was not the most productive in the sleep department. I'd turned on the light like a five-year-old kid scared of the monster in his closet and hesitated every time my eyes felt heavy to let them close. In all, I maybe slept for two hours that evening.

My meeting went smoothly, considering the sleepless night. Afterward, I decided to go to a bar and have a drink instead of going to my room right away. At the bar, I called home and chatted with my kids about their day, then I paid my tab and left.

Arriving back at the hotel, I hesitated at the door before inserting my key. I almost laughed at myself out loud. I was actually scared to put the darn thing in the scanner and open that door. But what did wait for me inside? Would there be anything to fear, or would it be completely normal, and I'd feel like a moron for worrying?

I held my breath, inserted the key, and this time, slowly opened the door and ventured my foot out in front of me in search of any objects blocking my path. There were none. I flipped the switch on in the room and squinted at the sudden brightness that fell around me. Everything looked just as I had left it. My bewilderment was short-lived as I made my way to my bed and kicked off my shoes. *See?* You must have completely overreacted, and stress must be causing you to be seeing and hearing things. Get a grip, man.

I tugged my sweaty socks off and walked over to the air conditioner and turned it on. It purred to life easily.

After a well-needed shower, I climbed into some comfortable clothes and pulled my laptop onto my lap as I sat in bed. I waited for it to come to life, but it did nothing. It was dead. I pecked at the power button frustrated, but it was to no avail. Still nothing. I'd plugged it in before I left for the day. How odd.

I leaned over and checked the power cord, and it was plugged into the wall alright. I attached the other end in my laptop, hit the power button, and my laptop came to life. I scratched my head. Hmm… Okay… that doesn't make much sense. Hopefully, this isn't a repeat of last night's unusual behavior.

Adjusting the cord slightly, I settled back against the headboard with my laptop sitting in my lap. I scrolled through some documents for a few hours and made notations where needed. Soon my eyes begged me for rest, and I abandoned the laptop on my nightstand and turned off the light. I'm not sure how long it took for sleep to come, but it was not very long at all.

I woke at two in the morning to sticky sheets and a sweat-soaked pillow. I listened for the loud hum of the air-conditioner, but like the night before, it had fallen silent. I sat upright in bed and felt a sudden ping of déjà vu. My eyes pierced the darkness for some sort of sign of life from the machine, but again, the green light was absent.

I thrashed at the sticky sheets, until they nestled at the foot of my bed, then pulled up only the comforter. I rolled onto my side, facing the air-conditioner, and tried to go back to sleep. Tonight, I didn't have the energy to get out of bed. I imagine I was silently not wanting a repeat of the previous night's events.

As sleep was washing over me, I began to succumb, that is, until the sensation of someone getting into bed with me occurred. My heavy eyes flashed wide open, and I laid there on my side frozen as the bed lightly adjusted against something or someone's weight. My veins ran frozen with icy blood, and my heart pounded insanely fast, so much so it throbbed in my eardrums.

I wasn't sure what to do. Do I turn around? Do I lay here and fall asleep anyways? Is this all in my mind? Am I really even awake? So many thoughts swarmed inside me, but I chose the bravest of them all and turned over in bed to see if anything was in bed beside me.

I let out a sigh of relief as nothing appeared on the bed. Upon searching the bed footboard to headboard, my sudden relief was replaced by pure terror. The bed was indented as if someone were lying beside me even though there was no visible form there. And on the pillow beside me was a sunk in spot about the size of a human head.

I scooted myself slowly back towards the wall so I could attempt an escape from whatever was in bed with me. I took my time, even though I was not sure how much I had before something sinister may happen. Once I could feel the edge of the bed on my side, and the bed still visually indented from whatever laid upon it, I hopped up amazingly fast, ran passed the bed, drew the lock on the door, kicked a shoe in place to keep the door from shutting and stood in the hallway breathless.

The brightness of the hallway washed over me, and I slinked against the wall in relief. Slowly the wall drew me to the floor where I sat for quite a while trying to gain my wits. I was pretty sure I was staying in a haunted room. But did I believe in such things? No. How else could any of this be explained, though? It just couldn't.

Finally, light from the sunrise started to flood in the hallway from a window at the end of the hall. Now that morning was approaching, I felt some courage to re-enter the room. If anything, I would flip the light on, then open the shades and let the light flood in like holy water, let it cleanse the darkness away.

I drew to my feet slowly, mentally preparing myself for the light switch's location, kicked the shoe aside, and reached for the wall switch. Once the room bathed in artificial light, I sighed in relief and made my way over to the curtains and drew them wide open as well.

I investigated the bed first. There were no signs of it being disturbed other than where I had discarded some of the covers when I had awoken or from where I'd slept. I searched the room with quizzical eyes for anything else but found nothing out of the ordinary.

I relaxed my shoulders and grabbed some clothes out of my closet for the day, and did a light freshening up in the bathroom before packing all of my things back in my suitcase and loading them into the car. I was losing my mind with all of the unexplained things going on, and for the last night of my trip, I would stay elsewhere. I honestly didn't care where, as long as it was not there.

At checkout, I hesitated to mention anything, but since the lobby was empty, I pried the lady slightly. "So… has anything weird ever been reported in the room I was staying in?"

She pecked at the keyboard but paused a moment to study my face, "Define weird."

My brow furrowed. How much detail would sound crazy at this point? I was not sure, so I trod lightly. "I think I heard footsteps and a few other things."

A smile creased the tips of her lips, and she nodded while continuing to type. "That's just Johnny. Occasionally he haunts the third floor. From what I hear, he's pretty harmless."

35 Paranormal follower

For my birthday, because I loved watching paranormal television shows, my boyfriend signed us up for a local paranormal investigation event at an abandoned and seemingly haunted asylum.

Since I could remember, I had wanted to try a ghostbox or voice recorder and ask questions in hopes of getting some kind of paranormal response. I guess part of me was just curious, and the other part was hopeful of some personal sign that there was life after death.

Let me give you some history. When I was eight years old, I lost my father in a car crash. It was sudden and quick they told us. He probably didn't feel a thing. I think they told us that to make it hurt less. But nothing hurt as bad as knowing that one day, your dad was there going on your field trips with you and the next, all of those trips were now distant memories. There would be no new ones.

Since my dad passed away, I dealt with the loss the best that I knew how. When I hit around fourteen, I watched my first paranormal television show and I was hooked. I had to know more. Then it just became a passion of mine, I guess.

For my birthday, my boyfriend bought me a voice recorder. When I unwrapped the gift, I turned the voice recorder over in my hands and looked up at him with questioning eyes. That's when he pointed to the envelope, which I greedily opened.

Inside were two tickets to a haunted asylum ghost hunt. I jumped out of my chair, threw my arms around his neck and started squealing in glee.

Not only was I going to see a haunted asylum, he had bought me a voice recorder! I was so excited!

My boyfriend Eric and I had been living together for about two months. We started dating our freshman year of college and six months later moved in together into a small two bedroom apartment fairly close to campus. It was a relationship that I anticipated leading to marriage after graduation.

The evening of the ghost hunt, we showed up about fifteen minutes early to the asylum. I climbed out of the car and zipped up my jacket. The wind had quite a chill to it.

The grounds of the asylum were weed infested. Overgrown plants and weeds intermingled to where there was no telling them apart. A sign announcing the asylum teetered on one side and squeaked in the wind as it hung by only one side.

The building looked quite massive in stature but its exterior was crumbling with age and neglect. The windows were empty except for the bars on the inside. The steps leading to the front enterance were also in need of repair. Pieces of crumbled concrete lay on both sides of the set of stairs. This building was in dire need of some TLC, for sure.

From behind me, I heard other vehicles approaching. Eric and I turned and shielded our eyes from the headlights as they parked.

The man in charge of the hunt, Charles, strode easily up the crumbling concrete stairs and stood just in front of the main entrance. He wavered there for a few minutes, watching everyone park and head towards the building. Once he thought everyone was within earshot, he welcomed everyone and went over the rules.

We were to stay together in groups of two at the least and not destroy any property. No smoking was allowed in the building either. After an hour, we were to regroup right inside the front door and share any paranormal findings with the group.

In front of us was a shallow set of stairs that led to the first ward. The frosted glass announcing the ward on the door was tinted grey from years of neglect.

I scanned the room slowly as we made our way up the stairs. I put my hand on the railing as I strode up the steps and pulled it back in disgust. Everything, including floors, railings and desks had at least an inch thick layer of dust on them. The walls appeared to orginally be a bright white but now were tinted a dirty beige.

The asylum was also stuffy. Probably from years of pent up dust and grime. The air was thick as well. Much thicker than the air from outside.

For the first fifteen minutes, nothing much happened. We walked through the whole first ward and to my dismay, we had spotted zero ghosts. I fished in my pocket for my voice recorder and decided to give it a whirl.

After I'd asked three or four questions, a door to our right slammed shut and then creaked back open ever-so-slowly. An echo from the door slamming seemed to thrive around the walls. It was if it repeatedly bounced up and down the hallway, refusing to cease. Eric and I looked at each other, nervously chuckled, and continued down the hall asking questions.

Once we'd entered the third floor ward, things began to happen more often. Each of these rooms did not have beds. They had gurnerys. I couldn't figure out why though. Was this a medical ward?

We ducked into one of the first rooms. Eric was asking questions while I snooped around. I put my finger on the counter by a lone sink in the corner and swiped it. A thick dust bunny stuck to my finger.

"Eww," Eric shook his head, "don't do that Kim. You don't know what's on that."

I nodded, shook my finger excessively until the dust bunny fell off and wiped the remainder onto my jeans.

From the hallway came thudding footsteps, as if someone were running. We looked at each other, eyes huge, and headed to the doorway to peak out into the hallway.

As expected, no one was there. "Must have been someone in another group or something," Eric said.

I nodded in agreement and we walked back out into the hallway towards the stairs leading to the fourth ward.

From behind us, we heard whispering. At first, it was very slow and barely audible. Then it grew faster and louder, but we had no idea what it was saying.

We turned in circles in the hallway, trying to decipher where it could be coming from, but neither of us could figure it out. Then, as suddenly as it had come on, it ceased.

Eric elbowed me in the ribs and I turned to glare at him. "What was that for?"

"Look down," he pointed at the dust covered floor. All was undisturbed except for bare footprints.

"Wait a second," I knelt down and got a better look. "Do you think these are from the running we just heard?" I tilted my head up towards Eric and watched him gulp.

"Ya, I think so."

"But why would one of the other groups take their shoes off?" I stood and put my hands on my hips.

"I don't think they were made by one of the other groups." I watched his eyes dart nervously around. "Maybe we should keep going?"

I was intrigued. I really wanted to linger in the hall and see what else we could conjure with our presence. But one look at Eric's sheet-white face told me he probably wasn't going to handle that very well, so I let him lead us up the fourth floor staircase.

I gazed at my watch. It told me we had about ten minutes before we needed to regroup at the front of the building. I held my arm up so Eric could see the time. He nodded in aknowledgement.

The rest of our excursion was uneventful. I'm pretty sure Eric was thrilled that there was no more phantom activity. However, I was a little bummed. I did have to say, for being my first ghost hunt, it had been a fun one. And it was definitely something I hoped to do again someday.

We regrouped at the front of the building and some had caught a word or two on their voice recorders. Some had heard scratching noises, others doors slamming just like us. We were the only group to see bare footprints or hear whispers though. It appeared that some of the others did not believe us when we talked about the sounds of running and then found bare footprints in the dust.

The whole ride home was quiet. I wanted to talk more about our experience but I could just tell Eric was worn out from the paranormal activity and wanted to let it go. So instead, I stared out the window at the dark trees that blurred by as we drove home.

The next morning, I was preparing a bagel with some cream cheese while Eric was showering before class. Then, a sudden overwhelming smell of cigarette smoke seemed to encircle me in the kitchen.

I hunted around towards the windows and the walls and even the front door, trying to find the source of the smell. Every place I went besides where I originally stood in the kitchen seemed to be fainter in smell. How could the smell be originating from where I was standing in the kitchen if I wasn't smoking?

Once Eric dressed, I asked him if he could smell cigarette smoke anywhere in the apartment. Amused he asked, "Why? Were you smoking?"

I gave him an annoyed glare. "Of course not."

"No, I don't smell any smoke. I'm going to be late though," he slipped a light jacket on and grabbed his car keys off of the counter, "I'll see you around four thirty."

I gave him a kiss and a big hug and watched as he disappeared through the door. Alone again, I sniffed the air. No more smell of cigarette smoke. Weird.

The whole next week was a blur of classes and tests. Eric and I weren't sleeping very well since some odd things would happen off and on in the apartment.

First, our golden retriever Doug would wake us up in the middle of the night barking in our room. He laid at the foot of our bed when he slept. But these nights, he'd be barking around two in the morning at a corner in our room. Sometimes, he'd even growl.

Then, the toilets started randomly flushing in the middle of the night. Not constantly, but every hour or two one of them would flush. Eric told me to have maintanence come look at it.

It wasn't until the next week that I realized that possibly something had followed us home from the ghost hunt.

I was doing laundry while Eric was still in class. I heard our doorbell ring, so I threw all of the clean clothes quickly into a hamper bin.

I'd been waiting for a package from my mom for my birthday. I was excited when it finally arrived. After I signed for it, I shut the door and walked back towards the laundry room while in the midst of trying to open it.

When I walked into the laundry room, I froze and nearly dropped the package from shock. The clean clothes I'd put into the clean hamper were literally thrown around the room. A shirt even hung from the ceiling fan as it slightly rotated.

When Eric got home I told him about what happened. He just brushed it off, thinking I was exaggerating. I was absolutely not. How do clothes hop out of a bin on their own and end up thrown around the room when I'm the only one home? They don't.

It wasn't long, though, before Eric believed me. He'd gotten up before me the next morning because he had a very early class that day. When he'd gone into the kitchen to start a pot of coffee, he noticed every single cupboard and drawer were opened. Even the fridge. A container of milk was turned over, dripping all over the inside of the fridge and the floor beneath it.

Frantically he'd run into the bedroom and shook me awake. He made me get up and look at the disaster in the kitchen. I will have to admit it was pretty unnerving to wake up to that.

I got out my laptop and searched some ways that we could cleanse the house by ourselves and hopefully get rid of whatever had followed us home.

I ran to a local church down the street and got a vial of holy water. Then I ran to a witchcraft store in town and bought some sage for smudging.

When Eric got home from school, we lit the sage and repeated, "You are no longer welcome here, you need to leave in the name of the Father, the Son, and the Holy Ghost, leave now."

I used the holy water to draw crosses on the outside of every doorway, in the kitchen and in the laundry room, because so far that's where most of the odd things had happened.

After we cleansed the house, we did not have anything else occur. Our toilets even stopped flushing themselves in the middle of the night. I'm pretty sure something followed us home from that ghost hunt, but now it's gone.

36 The beggar

Two years ago I moved out of my parent's home and into my first apartment by myself. I was attending college part-time and working part-time at the local newspaper, so my days were pretty busy and I was usually not home until it was already dark.

On one particular evening, a few weeks after moving in, I was walking up to my apartment building at about 7pm with some take-out bagged up.

A homeless man who obviously slept behind the building came up to me and asked if I had any spare change. He reeked of alcohol and vomit. I couldn't help but feel sad for the guy. I did not offer him any change, but did bring him down some of my leftovers when I was done eating and that began one of the most influential friendships of my life.

I would always stop outside the building after work and look for the man so we could talk a little before I went inside just to see how his day had been. On occasion, my uppity neighbors would give me a dirty look while passing into the building, which I quickly shrugged off. After all, he was still a human being and deserved to be treated with some dignity. Just because his life hadn't turned out like theirs was no reason to cast him off like garbage.

After a month or so of becoming chums, I began cooking for the man. Well more so, I would cook dinner for myself but make enough for a second person. I would plate it up on a paper plate and walk it down to him and chat while he ate. This seemed to thrill him to no end.

Fast forward about three months. I had left late from work this particular evening because we had had a staff meeting about newspaper deadlines. It was nearly nine before I reached my apartment building. Annie, my friend from work, had walked home with me. Since neither of us had school or work the next day, we were going to watch some scary movies and order in some food.

Upon arriving, I noticed the homeless man throwing up near the alley. I held a finger up to Annie to signal I would be right back and went to check on him.

I jogged over to him, put my hand on his back and asked if he was okay. He just kept vomiting. Finally I was able to get a good look at his face and noticed blood around his mouth. My eyes scanned the ground to where he had been vomiting and I noticed the blood there as well.

Terrified, I called out to Annie to call 911. She ran into the lobby, got the security guard and they placed the call.

After another minute or two of vomiting, the man just collapsed into my arms and I slowly placed him on the ground. He was no longer breathing.

By the time the ambulance arrived he was gone. There was nothing they could do. I was so heartbroken. Even though I'd had so many conversations with this man, I had never asked his name. To this day, I have no idea. Breaks my heart, honestly.

After that, there was not a day that went by that I didn't pause outside the building to look for the man before remembering that he was gone. It was a habit that took me awhile to break and for reality to set in. He was not going to be there anymore. He was gone.

It took about a month before he didn't cross my mind all the time. Life had just started to get somewhat back to normal. That's when the activity started.

One night in particular I had to help write out three separate collumns with a co-worker and it had taken us until about ten to finish. I walked into my apartment, threw my keys on the table, hung my purse on a coat rack I have by the front door and went straight to the fridge to figure out what I could make myself that would take the least amount of effort.

Let me explain that my kitchen was not the largest. I was a college student and even though I had a part time job, it was the nicest place I could afford on my salary. To the left of the fridge was a little bit of counter space with a sink. To the right of my fridge were all of my cupboards. So when the fridge is fully opened you cannot get into a cupboard.

I grabbed out some ham and cheese and mayonnaise and decided to make myself a quick and easy sandwich. I nudged the fridge shut with my shoulder and turned to walk to the sink and froze. Every single cupboard was open.

I set down the sandwich supplies and went through the entire apartment checking closets, under beds, windows and locks. No one else was there.

Back in the kitchen, I hesitantly shut all of the cupboards and made myself the sandwich. I sat on the couch, turned the television on and tried my best not to think about the incident for the rest of the night.

It was another two days before I noticed anything else unusual. Again, I had just gotten home from work, but at a reasonable time this night. It was around six thirty and I decided just to heat myself up some chilli. I opened the can, put a pot on the stove, turned the burner on and emptied the chili into it.

I hurried off to my bedroom to change into some lounge shorts and a tank top while the chili heated up.

After about a minute or two, I went back into the kitchen, grabbed a wooden spoon out of a drawer and started to stir the chili. The first thing I noticed was its consistency and I assumed I must not have turned the burner high enough.

I reached for the dial and noticed it was in the off position. Well that was weird. I shook my head, assuming I must have forgotten to turn the dial. I turned it on at a six and sat on the couch to watch some news while it warmed up.

During the first commercial break, I again walked over to the stove to check the chili. Again, the burner was off. At this point I was seriously thinking that I was losing my mind.

I removed the pot from the burner, turned the burner on at six again and waved my hand over the top. There was definitely heat coming from the burner, so the stove was working.

I placed the pot back on the stove and stood in front of it the whole time while it warmed, slowly stirring it.

Then, as I was stirring and listening to the news in the background, I heard it. I was a tiny click. I looked from left to right to try to figure out where the noise came from and noticed the burner dial was at "off" again.

Frustrated, and assuming this was the best I was going to get from my stove tonight, I pulled the chili off of the burner and spooned the lukewarm mixture into a bowl. I grabbed a spoon and sat back on the couch to finish the news.

That night, I was in bed reading one of my crime novels. My eyes were starting to hurt and droop, so I put my book on my nightstand, turned off my light and rolled over on my side.

Just as I was drifting off, there was tapping on my window. At first, I thought it was just a tree limb in the breeze. Then I remembered there were no trees outside of my apartment window.

More awake now, I started listening for it to happen again. It did after a minute or so. Just gentle sounds of tapping. Almost as if someone was outside my window poking it with a finger. But that would be impossible. I was on the third floor and there was no balcony or stairs outside my window.

After a few deep breaths, I convinced myself to go look out the window. As expected, there was nothing there. Just as I was letting go of the curtain and turning to head back to bed, the tapping happened inches from my face.

I felt like the blood had drained from my body and I was trying not to shake. A shapeless blob, static and dark was floating around outside of my window.

I let the curtain fall back into place, raced over to my night stand, turned my lamp on and tried my best to stay up most of the night. I finally passed out from exhaustion around one in the morning.

With more clarity the next day, I started to play the incidents over in my mind. The more I thought about them, the less scared I was.

All of the weird things happened after the homeless man passed away. I was pretty sure this was him. Was he telling me hello from the other side? Or was he trying to get my attention for other reasons?

Over the next few years, stuff happened off and on. Usually subtle things, nothing ever scary. The window tapping was probably the scariest of them all. I have seen the shadow figure quite a few times (the one I saw outside my window that night). I have to wonder if he will ever cross over or if he just wants to live with me forever. I never knew his name, so I dubbed him John.

Some nights I will just talk with John after he shows me that he's around. He seems to like that I think.

37 A twinly goodbye

My twin brother passed away from rare kidney disease. He and I were very close. I wouldn't say we were as close as best friends, but as teens, we did tell each other nearly everything.

The whole thing was so sudden, from being diagnosed to dialysis, then very fast downhill from there. There hadn't been enough time to even gain momentum on the donor list.

He was fifteen. We were identical in every sense except gender. Every time I looked in the mirror, I felt like part of him was staring back at me, and I broke down in uncontrollable sobs. Part of me wondered if there would ever be a day from this point forward that I would look in the mirror and not curse myself for looking just like him.

The morning of the funeral was slow going. I took a shower that seemed to take up ten times more energy than usual. Most everything I did that morning felt like my body was carrying concrete slabs behind me. It was such a chore to get dressed, brush my teeth, make my bed…

While brushing my hair in front of my dresser mirror, my tabby cat Felix hopped up and sat there watching me for a few moments. I watched him through the dresser mirror as I worked on a few knots in my wet hair.

All of a sudden, I noticed Felix eyeing the wall behind us. Then all of the hair on his back seemed to stand on end, and I'm sure my eyes grew larger. I'd never seen his hair stand on end before. I assumed it meant he was scared, but I couldn't be completely sure, so I just continued to observe him.

Felix stood up and arched his back, ready to pounce at some invisible force. From the mirror, the room was completely empty. I could not see a single thing out of place in my room that could be antagonizing him.

While watching through the mirror, the wall behind us began to slowly , and I leaned towards the mirror for clarification or a better look. I'm honestly not sure which.

It started off as a shadow, one that could possibly be defused by the sunrise outside on the odd shape of my bedroom curtains until it couldn't. It became larger and moved against the ivory wall towards my bedroom doorway.

At this point, I was starting to get as freaked as my cat. I whipped around to face the wall before the shadow could slip away from sight.

Drawing slow steps closer to it, I could feel a small electric pulse radiating from it. A shudder cast goosebumps up and down my arms. I rubbed at them with a terrified curiosity.

After four or five steps forward, I was within arm's reach of the mass. As if feeling threatened by the proximity, it exploded into what seemed like thousands of holographic, black particles, then completely disappeared.

The whole experience had me on edge most of the day. The funeral was the hardest thing I'd ever have to do in front of family. It took everything I had to compose myself. Once the eulogy had ended, I excused myself to the bathroom, and inside a stall broke into heart-wrenching sobs for nearly a half-hour.

After hugs, handshakes, and tears, my mother found me in the bathroom and helped me to the car. The drive home was so quiet; we were all mute. I was stuck in my head, reliving all of the memories I had gained from fifteen years of my brother's life, and I'm sure they were doing the same.

We finally got home around two in the afternoon, and I went straight to my bedroom with Felix. I laid on my bed, with him on my lap, turned on the television to some channel that I really didn't even care to watch and stared up at the ceiling while we cuddled in silence.

I'm not sure how long it took me to fall asleep, really. I know that my eyes were heavy and puffy from all of the crying, and after a time, I could not keep them open, and I just drifted off.

In the middle of the night, I awoke to a hissing noise. I glanced at the clock, unsure of what day or time it was. It was three in the morning.

Felix's back was arched, and he appeared to be hissing at a black mass standing at the end of my bed. The silhouette did nothing intimidating but wavered for a while as if it was watching us.

I eventually threw the covers over my head while Felix continued to growl and hiss at it. After about five minutes under my blanket protection, I pulled the blanket down just below my eyes… very cautiously.

There was no sign of the mass, and Felix was curled up sleeping again next to me. I half wondered if I had imagined it all.

The next morning, I awoke and just laid in my bed, cuddling Felix. Felix purred and rubbed his head against me.

I turned my head towards the drawn curtains and the sunlight trying to escape from their sides into my room.

I leaned up and opened them. I'd had enough grief and darkness; I felt ready to let some light into my life and my room.

As I pulled open the curtains, and the light cascaded over my entire room, my radio turned on behind me on my desk. The exact words on the song said, "Everything is going to be alright."

I half sat, half squatted on my bed in shock, peering over my shoulder, one hand still on one of my drapes.

Then the radio turned itself off. In shock, I scanned the room with my eyes and let my hand fall from the curtain.

Felix was sitting upright and seemed to be assessing the room for threats as well.

After a few minutes, I calmed myself and wrote it off as just a rare fluke of my radio. It was old; I'd had it since I was eight. Maybe it had developed a short or something?

As I made my way out of bed and eased my bare feet into my amazingly soft, fluffy slippers that I adore, the radio turned on again.

This time the words in the song sang, "I will always love you."

My knees buckled under me, and I fell to the floor on my butt and stared up at my desk in horror, shaking.

Again, the radio just shut itself off.

It was time for me to add up all of the events in my head. Two masses yesterday, two songs today. Was this my brother trying to communicate with me?

Then, as if in response to my inner thoughts, the radio played the lyrics, "You're still the one I run to, the one that I belong to, you're still the one I want for life."

My jaw dropped, and the tears just came like hot arrows from my eyes, cascading down my cheeks.

I can't say for sure over the last six years if this was, in fact, my brother communicating with me. However, I don't know how else to explain those two days.

After the third radio incident, it never turned on by itself again. I never saw a mass in my room or on my walls. It was as if he was saying goodbye and had to make sure I knew it was him before he could cross over.

38 You will be fine

I had a dream that made my blood run cold. Nothing like this had ever happened to me before in my life.

I loved my grandparents dearly, but with a crazy college class schedule to tend to and a part-time job, I was only able to keep in touch with them about once a month.

It was a Thursday night. I had just finished a shift at the local retail store I worked at, and I was exhausted. I watched a little TV and then dozed off in bed.

I only remember parts of the dream I had, but what I do remember is disturbing enough.

I'm standing in an empty parking lot with my grandfather. The moon is almost completely blanketed by clouds, and there is one lone streetlight about ten yards away.

From the limited light, I can make out some of my grandfather's features, but not all of them. He is standing about six feet away from me. his head turned towards the black sky, glancing up at the tiny sliver of moon that can be seen.

Suddenly, without notice of thunder or lightning, it starts pouring with rain. I throw my hands above my head in an attempt to shield myself from the droplets. I watch as my grandfather continues to stare up at the sky, rain running down his cheeks and drenching his short white hair.

Finally, after what seems like forever, my grandfather turns to look at me. He blinks rain droplets out of his eyes and smiles, then waves.

I hold my hand up and wave back.

He slowly saunters over to me, scoops me up in a big hug, and kisses my forehead.

"You will be fine," he says as he pulls away and searches my face for some sort of understanding.

I look up at him, terrified, although I'm not sure why. "Will I be?"

Again, he nods, rests his chin on the top of my head as we are both impaled by the droplets. "You know you will be."

I burst into tears that, after only a moment or two, turn into hysterical sobs.

He pulls back, puts my chin in his hand, and smiles into my eyes before turning and walking in the opposite direction of the streetlamp.

I watch him leave, my stomach lurching with every uncontrollable sob. Once the darkness has swallowed him, I drop to my knees in the pouring rain and cry some more.

At that point I woke myself up. I was sweating, and the dream lingered an echo in my ears.

I lay there in bed, staring at the ceiling, trying to pull myself free from the dream and back to reality. *Everything's OK; I'm OK, grandpa is OK.*

I took a deep breath in, reached for my cell phone, and checked the time. My heart stopped as my screen illuminated three missed calls from my grandmother.

I called her back, confused and speechless. She explained my grandpa had passed away in his sleep, very suddenly; that they thought it was a heart attack.

I fought the lump in my throat that seemed to rise with every word she said. My heart felt like it was being torn in small shreds.

My grandmother hung up, and I lay there again, staring at my ceiling. This time, I let the dream wash over me, and I cried silent sobs letting everything sink in.

Had my grandfather come to me in my dreams to say goodbye? To this day, I'm not sure how it is possible, but I think he did.

39 Marbles

I am not one to frighten super easily. I would like to say I try to figure out if there is a logical reasoning to something before I draw a conclusion. However, in 2005 my husband, myself, our five-year-old son Charlie, and our four-month-old daughter Samantha moved into a two-bedroom, one-bath apartment that had me climbing the walls from fright not too long after our arrival.

Our son had his own bedroom, and we chose to let the baby sleep in our room with us. I prefer that anyway until they are a little bit older. I tend to be the protective mom, with some occasional coddling.

In the middle of the week is when it started. We had only been at our new apartment for a few days, and I had had a short day at work, so I went home to shower before picking my son up from school. A feeling nagged at me my entire shower; it was as if someone were watching me. It made my skin crawl so bad that I decided to cut my shower short just to get out of the bathroom.

Another day after work, I ran home to fold the laundry and put it away before picking my son up from school. My husband was home unexpectedly working in the front room on his laptop. I stood in the hallway, folding items and putting some towels and things away in the hall closet. Out of the corner of my eye, I saw a figure come out of the front room as if it were going to approach me in the hallway. I assumed it was my husband.

I turned to face where I saw the figure, but there was nothing there. Then I had cold chills run down my body and give me goosebumps. At the same time, I felt a burning sensation on my arm as if I had been touched by something very warm. Not scalding by any means, but noticeable that it was warmer than a normal touch.

"Jessie?" I rubbed my arms with my hands and slowly walked to the edge of the hallway.

"Yes, Baby?" His voice floated from the front room.

I was stumped. He was still working away on his laptop. So, what I had just seen could not have possibly been him. Dumbfounded and a little unnerved, I made up a response. "Never mind, I found it!" And I turned back to my shortened pile of laundry and hastily put it all away just so I could be somewhere else other than in the hallway.

My son grew to fear the hallway as well. After a few months, he refused to use the bathroom at night. So, he would either wet the bed or urinate in his trash can in his room. After some time had passed, I bought a night light for the hallway in hopes it would make him feel safer, but it did not. The bulb burnt out after the first day. I assumed it possibly was a defective night light, so I bought a new bulb and installed it, but it would only last a day or two before burning out again.

Finally, I broke down and bought a different night light and continued having the same problems. A few days would go by, at the most a week, and the bulb would be useless. It confused me to no end. Especially because when the night light went dead, the bed-wetting started up again and I was washing bedding all the time. It got so bad eventually that I bought multiple sets of sheets for our son's bed. We even had to replace his mattress twice during our duration at this apartment.

The creepiest thing that happened to me in this house happened while my husband was away for a two-day work trip. I let my son sleep in bed with me, so all three of us were in one room. I awoke at around three in the morning to what sounded like someone dropping a handful of marbles onto the hardwood at the foot of my bed. I crept to the edge of the bed and looked down, expecting to see something dropped. There was nothing. So, I laid back against my pillow and laid there for a while, trying to convince myself whatever it was had just been a dream.

Just as I was beginning to doze off, my alarm radio on my bedside table went off at full blast. We did not even use it as an alarm. We used it for just the time in the mornings. I jumped out of bed so fast and ran for the light before silencing the radio.

When the room flooded with light, I switched off the radio and tried to slow my pulse. I checked on both kids, and luckily, they had slept through it. How, I have no idea. The volume had to have been on its highest setting.

I stood there by the side of the bed, trying to decide what to do. I was not quite sure what was happening, but something was. Should I take the kids to my mom's for the night? Would she think I was crazy for banging on her door in the early hours of the morning with both kids in tow? Surely that would make me look insane. We could go to a hotel, but then again, I would look like some unfit mother checking in with two kids in the middle of the night. So ultimately, I decided to stay and, if need be, lock my bedroom door and sleep with all the lights on.

The next afternoon my husband returned from his trip, and I told him I wanted to move. I had had enough of this place; it was creeping me out. Naturally, there was some push back because he is a total non-believer in things such as ghosts, and I was furious. I was starting to have a hard time sleeping because I feared something would happen, or I worried for my son, who usually slept by himself. Would it do something to mess with him in the middle of the night? And what was "it" anyway? Was it a ghost? I was not sure of anything.

Our last night in the apartment was one that dumbfounded my husband to the core. It was nearly midnight, and I was in the shower. Yes, one of those I feel like I am being watched the entire time showers. My husband was lying in bed reading when he started hearing a scratching sound under the bed like fingernails accompanied by a slight scurrying sound. Originally, he assumed maybe it was a mouse, so he bent over the side of the bed and drew up the bed skirt to find absolutely nothing. Then while he was still bent looking underneath the bed, our bedroom door slammed awfully loud. I could hear it through the noise of the shower. I promptly turned off the water, then hastily threw on a towel and went to see why my husband had slammed the door so loud when our children were sleeping.

I found him sitting in the middle of the bed, chewing on his fingernails and staring at the end of the bed.

"Why on earth are you slamming doors at midnight?" I harshly whispered at him, hastily grabbing my pajamas out of my dresser drawer.

He stared forward, barely moving, fingertips still in his mouth, "I-I didn't."

I threw my clothes on rather quickly and stood in front of him at the foot of the bed. "What do you mean you didn't? I heard it! In fact, all of us probably heard it!"

Finally, he drew his gaze up to meet mine, and I could see the shock and uncertainty painted all over it, and I knew then. He finally believed me.

Within three weeks, we had a new place to move to and we left that one behind. It was the worst experience of my life in that house. Even though things happened, I never did see what it was that was haunting us. But luckily, whatever was there chose to stay behind and not follow us.

40 The blue house

When I was really little, before I have any decently clear memories, we lived in this old blue colored house. My mom was sensitive to the paranormal, so she would constantly experience strange things.

One morning my father had gone off to work for the day, and I was asleep in my crib upstairs. She was in her bedroom getting dressed and heard clanking as if someone were washing the dishes in the kitchen.

Her first thought was to run to my room and check on me to make sure I was safe in case someone had broken in. Then she thoroughly checked the house to find no one, and the dishes remained in the sink, untouched and unwashed. There was no explanation for it.

Later on in the day, she was upstairs putting laundry away and heard footsteps climbing the stairs. Again, she was nervous and afraid. Her heart racing, she came out of her room with some fabric scissors and looked over the railing to see no one climbing the stairs, but the footsteps continued until they seemed to reach the top of the stairs and then stop.

When I was two, I adopted an imaginary friend. One who my mom swears was more ghostly than imaginary. I would talk to this entity in my room late at night. My mom would watch from the crack in the doorway as I jabbered at nothing.

A few months later, my mom was sick and in bed. My grandma had vowed to come over during the day and check on her. When my grandma arrived, she knocked, but no one answered.

Upstairs in her room, my mom heard the knocking, but when she tried to get out of bed, there was a sudden tension on both sides of the sheets, confining her to the bed. She kicked and wailed but for ten seconds or more, whatever it was had held her in place.

Finally, freed, she scooped me up out of my room and answered the door breathless.

My grandma was terrified by my mother's appearance upon answering the door and repeatedly asked my mother what was wrong. My mother was afraid my grandma would think she was crazy, so she tried to calm herself the best she could and explained she'd had a nightmare. My grandma was hesitant but eventually accepted the explanation.

My father did not always work super late, but on occasion, he did. During one of those times, my mom awoke to something pulling the covers off of her until they crumpled in a pile at the foot of her bed.

This happened more than once, as she can recall. Two of these times, she actually saw an apparition that appeared to be mid-thirties and female, with a crooked, slightly sinister smile on her face before disappearing into nothing.

When my mother had finally convinced my father to move, I was three. During the last week of the move, the closet in their room began to act up.

The door would slowly creak open in the middle of the night. This happened every day the last week. My father even witnessed it and, at that point, was thankful he'd agreed to move.

We have no answers as to what was in the house or why; just that it was an incredibly old home with possibly a long history and apparently quite the cast of spooks.

41 Ball of light

I was a person that was always fascinated with paranormal events. I always used to say things like, "I wish that would happen to me," or "Come on, that isn't that scary." I was ignorant of what it felt like to have an encounter of your own. All that changed a few months ago.

It began as any regular weekday evening would. My husband and I were sitting down in front of the television. He had an arm draped over me, and I snuggled in, enjoying his closeness. A commercial was on the television, and I was doing my best to ignore it.

From above me, light and movement caught my attention. I watched a small ball of light descend out of the ceiling and begin to hover in a small circle above the television. I looked over at Tim, expecting him to say something, to acknowledge the presence of the light, but he just stared blankly ahead, completely oblivious to what I was seeing. The ball was about the size of a softball, about 3.5 to 4 inches in diameter and just shone as if illuminated from within.

As I continued to stare at it, I felt a tingling sensation in my feet. My skin began to prickle as this vibrational hum began to slowly move up my body all the way to the top of my head. It was like a shiver was passing through my entire body but refused to relent. I sat there wanting to look away but somehow was compelled to stare at the orb. I am not sure I could have looked away even if I had tried.

I saw the television in my field of view, and it was like it was moving in slow motion. Whatever was happening to me seemed to be lasting for an eternity, but from what was on television, it had only lasted seconds. Mercifully, the humming began to subside. It moved down my body before finally disappearing in my feet. The orb hovered there for a few seconds then gracefully lifted back up into the ceiling from where it had come.

Suddenly it is like time snapped back to normal. The television was incredibly loud, and I had a high-pitched squeal in my ears. When I tried, the movements of my arms and legs felt jerky and unrehearsed. It felt as if I was coming out of a deep sleep, but that wasn't possible, I had been awake, and the experience had only lasted seconds.

My tongue felt foreign in my mouth as I tried to formulate words to ask Tim if he had seen the light. A frown creased his forehead as he looked at me with confusion and concern.

"What light?" he asked.

For some reason, I was angry

with him for questioning me. It had been right there in front of him. There was no way he could not have seen it. It was only a few feet away from him.

"Are you feeling okay, Hun?" He asked me as he placed the back of his hand over my forehead, trying to see if I felt warm.

I swatted his hand away in exasperation, "Yes, I'm okay! Now answer my question. Did you see that light above the television?"

I had surprised him with my sudden outburst, and he took his arm away from around my shoulders. "No, I didn't see any light!" He snapped back.

I do not know why, but his answer just made me even more angry that night. It was like he was acting like I was crazy and had made it up. I tried to calm down and explain what I had seen and felt to him. I saw several emotions pass over his face as I described what I had experienced from disbelief to concern.

In the end, I just had to accept that I was the only one that had seen anything.

I no longer readily dismiss what people say when they tell me about their own experiences. I don't know what the orb was doing to me, but I know I couldn't stop it. That feeling of powerlessness is something I will never forget.

42 Cemetery chills

Late one night, my friend Sarah and I were hanging out at her place when her mom Christin came up and asked us if we wanted to check out a graveyard. Both of us being fans of the supernatural we were more than excited for the opportunity to come in contact with something from the other side. We both grabbed a sweatshirt and jumped in Sarah's mom's car.

There are a few different cemeteries in our town, but one, in particular, is much older than the other two and has more than its share of stories of people seeing ghosts in the form of shadows or, on occasion, a full-bodied apparition. This cemetery was called Thorn Ridge. It was still in use, but it held graves from back into the mid-1800s. When we were asked what one we wanted to go to, the answer was simple; it was Thorn Ridge.

We had to drive about 45 minutes from her house to get to the cemetery. As we drove alongside one of the walls, we noticed a pair of headlights behind our car. Already a little on edge, we hadn't seen anyone follow us up the road leading to the gates. I could see a bit of a panicked expression in Christin's eyes as she continued to look back in the rearview mirror. Sarah and I, fueled by her mom's fear, had little trepidation when she decided to speed up in order to lose our pursuer. We turned quickly around the corner, crushing Sarah and me against each other in the back seat. Christin stopped the car and abruptly killed the lights. Darkness surrounded us as we all craned our necks behind, looking for our tail. Nothing came, though. Even if they turned around, the car behind us would have at least shown its lights moving. This did little to settle us as we waited a few minutes, thinking that we would wait the other car out, and they would just leave after growing impatient.

After we figured that if someone was coming, they would have done so by then, Christin turned the ignition on the car. All we heard was a clicking noise as the car refused to turn over. A cold shiver of dread crept down my spine as I imagined us being isolated out there. I nervously looked down at my phone to see what time it was. I pressed a button to bring up the screen, but it wouldn't turn on. I had at least 85% battery when we left, so there was no way that my phone could have died in 45 minutes. Meanwhile, Christin continued to try and get the car to start, but no matter what she did, the engine refused to turn over.

I squinted into the darkness outside, trying to see out my window. It was like I was in an ocean of blackness. Thorn Ridge doesn't have any lights on at night, so it was impossible to see clearly for more than a few feet. I saw in the distance what looked like a blur coming towards the car and pressed closer to the window straining to see what it was. All of a sudden, there was a loud and wet thwack on my window. I jumped out of my seat on top of Sarah from sudden terror. I looked at my window and could see a dark black smudge on the glass where something had hit it. Sarah, just as scared as I, was clutching me so hard that her nails had dug deep into my arms.

Slowly I reached out my hand and unlocked the door. The mechanical *thunk* it made was loud in the stillness of the car. I grabbed the handle, and before my courage failed, I pulled the lever and swung the door open. I looked to the ground, and there lay a small bird, its neck twisted at a grotesque angle, obviously broken. I felt my stomach lurch as I yanked the door closed, shielding myself from the gruesome sight.

Sarah asked me what it was. From the look on her face, it was obvious she didn't want to know.

Christin told me to stay in the car where she could see me. At that point, I didn't need an invitation; I wasn't going anywhere. From behind us, I heard a loud screech like nails scraping over the metal of the trunk. Too terrified to look back, I clung to Sarah, trying to find comfort in our closeness.

I looked up to the mirror and saw Christin's eyes go wide at what she saw behind us. She twisted the key again, and the engine finally caught. She dovetailed rocks and dirt as she slammed the pedal to the floor. The car straightened out, and we flew down the road. Only then did I find the courage to look back, but there wasn't anything there.
Sarah asked her mom what was behind us, and all we got was a whispered, "I don't know, Honey, I don't know."

When we got back to her house, we looked at the trunk of the car, and we saw four scratch marks in the paint deep enough to show the metal below.

I'm still interested in the paranormal to this day. That night on the road next to Thorn Ridge was the most terrifying moment of my life. To this day, I can't drive by it without a chill passing down my spine, and I never, ever, go there at night.

43 House of tragedy

A long time ago, when I was a child, we grew up next to a home that had a tremendously violent history. The first owners of the home were murdered by an escaped convict. The next couple to purchase the home did not remain married exceedingly long before their marriage ended in turmoil and tension. At one point, the wife had had enough and jumped from the upstairs window while holding her baby, killing them both.

One evening my parents were driving home, when a freak snowstorm occurred. Being unable to make the drive, they'd asked our neighbors to

care for us until they could finish their
journey home.

My brother and I knew full well of
the history of this home and were not
pleased at all of having to stay there.

At first, everything seemed calm
and normal. But not long after our arrival
did subtle things begin to occur.

To start it off, my brother and I
were watching television in their living
room not too long before bed. Then the
television began switching on and off
and glitching out.

We were slightly concerned,
exchanging nervous glances but
chalked it up to possibly the storm
messing with the power or something.

Then while in the bathroom
getting ready for bed, I was startled by
the sound of a glass shattering in the
shower. It sounded as if someone had
thrown it and it broke into a thousand
pieces. I ran to get Dale, the man of the
house, and made him check behind the
curtain. There was nothing behind it. No
glass, nothing out of the ordinary at all.

Having to go to bed at that point
and still shaken by the crazy glass
incident, I was on edge. I was to sleep
on our neighbor's couch that night and I

asked them to leave the kitchen light on so I would not be scared.

As I was starting to doze off, I heard the creaking of wood followed by a noticeably light thud here and there. I opened one eye suspiciously and peered around the room, and my gaze fell onto the rocking chair. It was rocking by itself. *Crrrrreeeeaaaakkkk... thudddd...*

My eyes were like saucers, and I was frozen in place. My brother lay across from me on the loveseat, already snoring away.

I pulled my blanket over my face and started to cry; I was so terrified. Under the blanket, I trembled and prayed for it to stop. After about ten minutes, the room finally fell silent except for the deep breaths of my brother sleeping.

It was exceedingly difficult to fall asleep after that. I laid there for what seemed like hours, still under the blanket, terrified to peek out. Finally, I dozed off.

In the middle of the night, I was awoken by the sound of footsteps coming down the stairs. For a moment, I pulled the blanket off of my face and scanned the room. My brother was awake as well and sitting upright listening to them.

We exchanged worried glances, and I motioned for him to join me on the couch, which he did almost immediately, and we shivered in fear while holding each other.

The footsteps reached the bottom of the stairs and then ceased. Although they dissipated, we both stayed huddled together for a good twenty minutes or more.

Finally, my brother went back to his loveseat and laid down, as did I. I don't know how long it took us to fall asleep, but we finally did until morning.

The next morning, we were both open and honest with Dale and his wife about what we had heard. I asked them how they could stay in such a creepy house, and they shrugged and said it was probably the house just settling, and they were used to it.

Thinking about it today just freaks me out as much as it did back then. At the very least, there was no explanation for the footsteps. I have never heard a house settle and have it sound like that before.

That was the creepiest night of my life. And you would be correct if you assumed I stayed as far away from their house as possible the rest of our time in that neighborhood. I'd even started walking to school the "long way" so that I didn't have to walk past their creepy haunted house.

44 Historical charm

We fell in love with a historical house that was built in the late 1800's. Upon buying it and moving in, we adored its charm and appeal.

After only one week in the house, we began to experience what we dubbed our "unseen friend."

For five years, we put up with numerous hauntings, trickery and activity. Some minor, some terrifying.

The first instance was during the summer in the middle of the night. The kids were out of school and able to be up late at night (to a degree).

On night, our son Paxton came bolting breathless into our bedroom around midnight. He demanded why we were running across the floor downstairs back and forth.

My husband looked at me speechless, as I looked at him confused. We had been in bed the whole time reading and were just turning out our light for the night.

I told him it hadn't been us. My husband, panicking, went to check on the noises while my son stayed in the room with me.

He checked the entire house. It was still pitch black, all the lights were still off, and everything was locked up tight.

He came back to the bedroom and shrugged, offering that maybe Paxton had a nightmare. My son was adamant that this was not a nightmare and that he hadn't even went to bed yet. I tried to calm him the best I could and walked him back to his bedroom.

Fast forward to late August. The kids had just resumed school and bedtimes were earlier now. It had to be around ten in the evening. My husband and I were reading the news on our phones. Suddenly, there was a loud thump, followed by two smaller thumps right outside our bedroom door.

Assuming it was one of our children out of bed, my husband went out of the room to catch them in the act. He was shocked to find the hallway pitch black and silent.

Confused, he went down the hallway to see if one of them ran back to their room to avoid getting into trouble for being up past bedtime. All three of them were sound asleep.

A few months later, we were getting ready for Thanksgiving. We were preparing all of the smaller dishes the night before so that the oven wasn't so crowded for the main dishes.

I had just finished wrapping the last of the pre-made dishes and put them in the fridge. My husband was sitting on the sofa watching television. I took off my apron, hung it up and went to join him on the couch.

Suddenly, the back door swung open loudly and slammed shut. At first, we just accepted it was one of the kids coming in because it was starting to get dark outside.

My husband yelled, "Don't track mud in the house, and don't slam the door!"

When there was no response, I went to check the mudroom, and no one was there. I peeked out the window beside the door and all three were still playing and laughing in the backyard.

The night before Christmas, my husband and I finished putting out all of the kids' presents. We were exhausted. We had to build this and that so it was easier for the kids in the morning.

Instead of reading, we decided to go straight to bed. My husband fell asleep before I could and started snoring loudly as usual.

I was overcome with a feeling of being watched. I just couldn't seem to shake it. I heard the sound of creaky floorboards right at the foot of our bed.

Completely frozen in place and freaking out, I tried my best to nudge my husband awake. He continued snoring on unphased.

I pulled the blankets over my head and listened in between my husband's snores. The creaking sounded as if it was moving to my side of the bed. I was too freaked out to lower the covers.

I held my breath and tried to nudge my husband again. Nothing. Still snoring. At this point, I was absolutely terrified. My heartbeat was literally ringing in my ears.

Suddenly, it was as if a wind was on the other side of the blanket. Or maybe a breath? The blanket ripped away from my fingers slightly in front of my face. I continued to hold my breath and squinted with my eyes closed. Then I heard the lowest whisper, "I see you."

Over the years, there were many more happenings in our home. Thankfully, the bedroom incident was the worst that ever happened. After that incident, I made sure that I fell asleep before my husband.

45 The boat

My mother Elena suffered from epilepsy. She had it as long as I could remember. Now grown and on my own, I felt it was my duty to take her in and keep an eye on her. You never knew when she would have a seizure and there's no known cure for it.

Some people are lucky and only have it occur for a few years, while others have it their entire lives. My mom was an unfortunate case.

It was around two in the morning, and a clatter coming from my mother's room woke me up.

Hastily, I ran to investigate. My mother was tangled in her bedding, obviously having a seizure and suffocating. I did my best to untangle her while dialing 911.

I performed CPR on her until paramedics arrived. Once they were in the house, I felt like I was in an ant farm. People were running here and shuffling there. I was shoved out of the way so they could work on her. I was numb. Delirious and numb.

I sat on the bottom stair, which was right outside her bedroom, and just stared off into space. The only thought I could recollect is *this better not be how it ends. This cannot be how it ends.*

After a few minutes, which almost felt like hours, paramedics got her breathing again. Immediately, they transported her to the hospital.

I stayed behind to get dressed. I was still in my boxers with no shirt on.

In my room, still numb, fumbling through my drawers for something quick and easy to throw on, the phone rang. It was my aunt.

I answered thoughtlessly, still exhausted.

She was breathless and sounded groggy. "Jake, you will not believe the dream I just had. I had a dream that I was on a boat with your mother. We were sailing off into the golden bright sunset and then she turned to me and told me she was dead. It felt so real."

I choked on her words and just sat there in silence. I stared at the wall in front of me. I knew. Well, I was fairly sure I knew. This was too much of a coincidence to not have some truth.

I told her what had just happened and she agreed to meet me at the hospital immediately.

I tugged on my shoes, grabbed my keys and drove in a blur to the hospital.

As I expected, the doctor was waiting for me when I arrived. His facial expression told me all I needed to know. She was gone.

The chaplain escorted my Aunt and I to a room and to console us. I know I was supposed to feel better after talking with him, but I didn't.

I sat there with my elbows on my knees, my head in my hands and tried to stay calm. I tried to make sense of the words being directed at me. But I felt like I was trying to understand Charlie Brown's teacher. None of it made much sense.

I didn't get home until around six in the morning. The horizon was already peeking light throughout the valley.

I threw my keys in my key dish and landed with a belly-flop on the couch. There was no need to sleep in my bed, this would do simply fine.

I grabbed the blanket off of the back of the couch and tucked myself under it, as if hiding from the world would shield the pain I was feeling. The absolute shock and loss was overwhelming my entire body.

Soon I drifted off. I dreamt of an ocean. The water's edge was highlighted by golden sunlight. It was beautiful.

Birds cawed in the distance and the lapping noises of the ocean were

soothing. I was on a boat. *The* boat.
My Aunt's boat.

My mom sat next to me smiling,
watching me be mesmerized by the
water and the sky. She put the back of
her hand up and grazed my cheek.

"I guess you know," she said and
stared off into the sunset.

"I guess I know," I replied.

46 Name calling

My parents divorced when I was ten. I suffered from severe anxiety and depression. In the midst of dealing with my mental health, strange things began to happen at home.

One night I was up late, about one a.m. in the morning. I was having trouble sleeping on some of my medications. I was watching television quietly as to not bother my mom.

All of the sudden, I heard a man's voice say my name. I sat there for a few minutes and heard nothing more, so I brushed it off and eventually went to sleep.

A few nights later, I was up late again, having trouble sleeping. Again, I was watching television and it was around one o'clock in the morning. I heard someone call my name again, this time louder and closer. It was as if whoever said it was standing in the doorway of my room.

I turned on my side lamp and saw no one. I went to my mom's room and they were both sleeping. I fought off a shudder and went back to my room and shut the door.

It was a few days before anything else happened, so I had forgotten all about my name being called.

Lounging in my bed, snacking on some chips, it was around midnight. I had my door very lightly cracked instead of open, like I usually leave it.

The door began to creak and open by itself. Then the room had to drop of at least ten degrees in temperature. I sat there holding a chip up to my lips, just staring at the door.

Then I heard what sounded like scuffing footsteps on the hardwood floor towards my bed. They weren't normal "thump, thump" steps. It was like someone was sliding their shoes or feet on the floor as they walked.

I kept eyeing the door and there was nothing there. No ghostly figure, no mist, nothing. But still I heard the scuffling getting closer to my bed.

I finally jumped out of bed and ran out into the hallway, screaming for my mom.

She ran out into the hallway frazzled, and took me under her arm and held me. She led me back to my room (which was the last place I wanted to be) and told me there was nothing to be afraid of.

This activity went on for years. My mom didn't believe me, my dad thought I was making it up. They thought I was just acting out because of the divorce or it was some sort of side effect of the medication I was on.

They had my doctor prescribe some sleeping pills to help me fall asleep and that helped somewhat. I guess it was better to sleep through whatever was happening than be awake for it.

It was about two years before I quit hearing the voice calling my name in the middle of the night. My mom got relocated to a different city with her job and it stopped.

I never told her about it, mostly because I started thinking that I was crazy.

47 Eyeless

Our old house was spooky. There was no doubt in my mind.

In the beginning, the activity was minor. My keys were moved from where I had left them on the table or floorboards would creak behind us while watching television.

But one night, I had to work late. I came home and relieved the babysitter. Then I went into my daughter's room to tuck her in.

She was sound asleep. I gave her a kiss on the head and headed to my bedroom to take a shower before bed.

Once in the shower, I heard a scratching noise. It was like branches on a window. The only thing is, my bathroom doesn't have a window.

So, I opened the shower door and peered out to see if my daughter had gotten out of bed or see what she was doing. I did not see anyone.

I decided to turn the water off and get out of the shower so I could further investigate.

Once in my room dressing, I heard the noise again. This time it sounded like it was coming from the hallway.

I hastily threw my shirt on and went out into the hallway. Again, nothing.

I was pretty rattled and confused at what was happening. This noise was not something I had ever heard in my house before.

I decided to check on my daughter again in case someone broke in or something. She was tucked in the corner of her bed, whimpering.

I started asking her, over and over, what was wrong. But she just kept staring at a corner of her room towards the ceiling, then darting her eyes towards me and back to the ceiling. Her eyes were filled with pure terror.

I made my way over to her, sat on her bed, and took her into my arms. I started rocking her and putting my fingers through her hair, telling her everything was going to be ok.

"Did you have a nightmare honey?" I asked.

She pointed towards the ceiling in the corner with a shaky finger and said, "Don't you see the man with no eyes right there mommy?"

My eyes about bugged out of my head. I hadn't turned on any lights in her room. Her room was only softly illuminated with a night light.

I had to be the protector. So, I slowly turned my head in the direction of her finger and looked at the ceiling. I did not see a man with no eyes, but I did see a black mist up by the ceiling.

I scooped my daughter up and brought her into my room. That's where we both slept with the door locked (like it would have kept out a spirit).

For several years, my daughter has told me about the man with no eyes. She says he does nothing to harm her. He just stares at her in the middle of the night. Sometimes he's on the ceiling and sometimes he is in her closet.

48 Scared to death

     I worked at night as a 911 operator. On this particular day, I received the weirdest call of my career.

     A woman called in around two in the morning, terrified. She said there was a ghost in her house and her and her daughter were terrified to leave the bedroom to get out of the house.

     In the background of the call, you could literally hear things smashing in the distance. I'm not one to believe in ghosts, so this call threw me for quite the loop.

I dispatched help to their location and kept asking her if it was possible that an intruder had broken in. She kept telling me no. She was sure. She had seen the thing and so had her daughter. She said, stoically, that it was not of this world.

I tried to keep her calm until help arrived. But then she started screaming that it was now at their bedroom door jangling the doorknob and that it was going to get in.

Again, I was saying anything I could to keep her calm. Then I could hear the sound of the doorknob falling on the floor and I heard her draw in a breath and whisper, "Oh my god."

Then the line went dead.

I asked for an update after emergency crews arrived. It still spooks me to this day.

They had to break in the front door because everything was locked. No intruder was in the house.

They found the mom and daughter in the bedroom. The daughter was whimpering under the bed, while the mom was deceased on the floor.

The doorknob was laying right inside the bedroom on the floor.

When they asked the daughter what had happened, she said, "It was the scary man who only appears at night."

The mom died of Broken Heart Syndrome. So basically, the woman was scared to death. It still gives me chills to this day.

49 Slammed

I was on the phone with my child's insurance company. My baby was in his crib in the bedroom asleep as I paced the living room with the phone up to my ear.

The bedroom door was open so I could periodically check on him while I was on the phone.

At this point, I had been on hold for about ten minutes and was starting to get agitated regarding the amount of time I was having to hang on.

Out of the corner of my eye, I saw a black figure glide across the hallway and into my son's room. With a quizzical look on my face, I kept the phone to my ear and went towards my son's room to investigate.

The minute I arrived at his doorway; the door slammed shut in my face. I threw the phone on the floor and began hastily trying to turn the knob on the door. It would not turn!

I ran to the adjoining bathroom. My hands at this point were shaky and sweaty, but the door was not locked and, after two tries, I was able to get the door open.

Once in the room, I noticed my son had woken up but was not crying. He was staring at the door that had slammed shut with a curious look on his face.

I scooped him up to check him out. He was completely fine. I glanced around the room while holding him close and saw nothing amiss.

Although there was nothing in there, the air was heavy. And I had an extremely creepy feeling something was watching me.

I walked over to the door that had slammed shut and locked. However, the lock was in the position of being unlocked. I grabbed the handle and turned it. It opened simply fine.

50 Vacant

It was my birthday weekend. I had begged my parents to let me invite over a few friends and tent camp in our backyard. I was ten after all, and big enough to be in the backyard with a few friends for just one night.

Hesitantly, my mother agreed. My father was to check on us multiple times throughout the evening just to make sure everything was going smoothly.

My house was literally two houses away from an old cemetery built in the late 1800's. And I was determined to get a rise out of my friends by telling ghost stories.

In the late afternoon, I helped my father set up the tent. He kept reminding me to stay in the yard and no funny business because he would be checking on us at random times. I nodded and agreed. I had no intentions of leaving the yard.

My friends and I jumped on my trampoline for the next few hours. We went inside, grabbed some popcorn, some sodas and brought it back out to the tent and readied our beds.

As it began getting dark, my parents came out to say goodnight and make sure we all had that we needed in the tent for the evening.

When my parents went back inside, we turned on our flashlights and talked about some of the girls at school.

Brian was the scaredy-cat of the bunch and I was extremely excited to scare him with a really good story.

He kept telling us he was hearing rustling in the bushes. Eddie, my other friend, unzipped the tent once to check and there was nothing there.

We pretty much shrugged it off as Brian being scaredy-cat. Brian and I continued to chat awhile longer.

When it was really good and dark, I suggested telling ghost stories. Eddie was elated, while Brian gulped and tried to hide his wide, unsure eyes.

We patted Brian on the shoulder and assured him the stories would not be too scary. He nodded and agreed. We let him go first.

His story was not the best attempt and wouldn't have scared a toddler. Eddie and I kept exchanging bored glances and patiently waited for him to finish.

Once Brian had finished, Eddie and I faked shocked and patted Brian on the shoulder.

"Good one," I said. "Ok Eddie, your turn."

Eddie began a story about a vacant house on the outskirts of town where a little boy had died. The little boy's family moved away a few years after his death from the trauma. The little boy roamed the streets of the town searching and hoping to find his family.

This boy was not a nice little boy. He was angry with his family for leaving him to rot alone in the house forever. He would terrorize people on the streets late at night.

He would try and shove them in front of oncoming cars or trip them so that they would fall -- those types of things.

When Eddie was done, I gave him a thumbs up. "Good one dude."

Brian looked at Eddie and then looked back at me. He knew I was the best storyteller out of all of us. I'm pretty sure he was scared to hear what my story was going to be about.

Before I had a chance to start my story, however, the zipper on the tent slowly started unzipping itself.

All three of us sat there, flashlights pointed upwards at our chins in horror. We just listened as it kept unzipping, just slowly enough to hear.

I tried to calm down by telling the guys it was probably just my dad checking in on us. I got up to prove my point.

When I finished unzipping the tent and stuck my head out, no one was there. Quickly I pushed myself back into the tent and sat there frozen.

Both boys looked at me expectantly.

"Well?" Brian nudged big bulging eyes. "Is it your dad?"

With all my might, I shook my head no and sat there with my arms wrapped around my stomach.

"What are you waiting for then!" Eddie screamed, "I'm going inside!"

Both boys took off to my house, while I was following closely behind. I kept turning my head and glancing behind me for some person to be following at my heels.

The only thing I saw was at the gate of the cemetery. It looked like a little boy was standing there, holding a teddy bear in one hand while staring directly at us.

FROM THE AUTHOR

At any early age I knew I noticed things that others did not. That I had a sensitivity about me that I could not quite explain.

I loved all horror movies, paranormal movies or shows and grew to love what some others just didn't care to understand.

Through the years I have come to realize that I am what they call "an empath". I feel things that others don't. It could be a place, a thing, a location, or someone talking to me and I just know more is going on then what they claim.

Honestly, I do not do much about this in my life. I've learned to deal with it, and not use it for anything other than knowledge.

I have lived in two haunted houses. This got me interested in the paranormal world and to seeking answers of all shapes and kinds.

I recently started a podcast and we discuss almost everything paranormal, mysterious or unknown. Feel free to take a listen and share your own ghost experiences with us as well!

Forever Haunted Podcast

The Ghosts That Haunt Me with Eve Evans Podcast

A Truly Haunted Podcast

Follow Eve S. Evans on instagram @eves.evansauthor

4718266fF-8350-4a6b-b130-82e4dbf743cR01

Made in the USA
Monee, IL
01 December 2021